D0350665

NORMALLY, THIS WOULD BE
CAUSE FOR CONCERN

NORMALLY, THIS WOULD BE
CAUSE FOR CONCERN

Tales of Calamity

and

Unrelenting Awkwardness

DANIELLE FISHEL

GALLERY BOOKS

NEW YORK · LONDON · TORONTO · SYDNEY · NEW DELHI

G

Gallery Books
A Division of Simon & Schuster, Inc.
1230 Avenue of the Americas
New York, NY 10020

First Gallery Books hardcover edition September 2014

GALLERY BOOKS and colophon are registered trademarks of Simon & Schuster, Inc.

For information about special discounts for bulk purchases, please contact Simon & Schuster Special Sales at 1-866-506-1949 or business@simonandschuster.com.

The Simon & Schuster Speakers Bureau can bring authors to your live event. For more information or to book an event, contact the Simon & Schuster Speakers Bureau at 1-866-248-3049 or visit our website at www.simonspeakers.com.

Interior design by Jaime Putorti
Cover photograph © Paul Mobley Photography

Manufactured in the United States of America

10 9 8 7 6 5 4 3 2 1

Library of Congress Cataloging-in-Publication Data

Fishel, Danielle.
    Normally, this would be cause for concern : tales of calamity and unrelenting awkwardness / Danielle Fishel. — First Gallery Books hardcover edition.
        pages cm.
    1. Fishel, Danielle. 2. Television actors and actresses—United States—Biography.
I. Title.
    PN2287.F49A3 2014
    791.4502'8092—dc23
    {B}   2014020242

ISBN 978-1-4767-6023-0
ISBN 978-1-4767-6025-4 (ebook)

To having no limit. ∞

CONTENTS

Contents

NORMALLY, THIS WOULD BE
CAUSE FOR CONCERN

CHAPTER 1

WILL ACT FOR SHOES

Aside from a certain segment of A-list actors, most of us who act professionally don't have much, if any, control over what we work on and when we work on it. Considering that "Type A Personality" should be my middle name, this makes me crazy in the head.

Auditioning for a role you really want can be awful. You only have a few minutes in the room to show what you're capable of, and you might only have a couple of hours to prepare for it. You audition for a thousand more roles than you'll ever actually book, so there is a ton of rejection, and it isn't always about your performance. Is your hair color right? Is your weight right? Are you the right height? Can you walk and chew gum at the same time?

The problem is, you have no idea what the casting director, director, or producers are looking for, so you just have to walk in naked (figuratively; I don't suggest *actually* going in naked, but if you do, please let me know so I can laugh my ass off) and hope they love you.

Sometimes auditions are the opposite of what I've just described. The show or movie is fantastic, the casting director is incredibly kind, and you feel great about what you're doing. I wish I could say that's how my *Boy Meets World* (*BMW*) audition went when I auditioned for the role of Topanga. But it wasn't.

I started acting at ten, because when I was in elementary school there was a tall, gorgeous girl who was a year or two older than I was whom I really looked up to. That's not just a short-person joke; I actually wanted to be like her. She came to school one day and told me she had just signed with an agent and was going to be a model. She told me I could be a model, too.

That was all I needed to know.

"Mom," I said when she picked me up from school, "I want to be a model." She asked why, and I told her it was because Heather, the aforementioned tall, gorgeous girl at my school, was going to be a model. My extremely kind, warmhearted, and supportive mother explained to me that you have to be taller than four feet to be considered as a model in any capacity. I had been hoping that endless enthusiasm for posing in front of every camera I came across since the age of two would make up for my being vertically challenged, but . . . no. Hmmm. I hadn't anticipated a hang-up in my career path this early on.

I started my nonexistent modeling career at two years old.

I went to school the next day and told Heather the bad news.

"Ugh, my mom said that I'm too short to be a model," I lamented.

"Oh!" Heather said. "My agent is also going to put me on TV, and I don't think you need to be tall to be on TV."

She was right. You don't have to be tall to be on TV, and that was going to be my new goal. Forget the fact that starting a career in the entertainment industry is next to impossible, or that we lived fifty miles from Los Angeles, or that I didn't know the first thing about acting. I was going to make this happen.

Truthfully, my parents didn't want me to be an actor. They had only heard horror stories about former child stars, and I had to beg them for a year to let me get an agent and start audi-

tioning. They only relented because they figured I would probably get bored with auditioning before I would ever be lucky
enough to book a job and make the almost inevitable down-
ward spiral that plagues young Hollywood. Ha! Wrong. Well,
at least half wrong. Maybe my spiral is coming and my crazy
just hasn't kicked in yet. I still have time to ruin everything!

By age twelve, I had been acting for almost two years. I had
done several commercials and a couple of guest spots on TV
shows. None of these jobs required a whole lot of acting, because
they were parts where I was just a slightly exaggerated form of
my own naturally perky, carefree personality at that age. And
then I got the call for an audition for a new show called *Boy
Meets World*. The name of the episode was "Cory's Alternative
Friends."

The role I was auditioning for was Topanga. She was a young
"flower child" who was quirky and could possibly end up being
a recurring character. I went in for the audition and read the
lines exactly the way twelve-year-old Danielle would have said
them. I spoke fast, with too much energy, and guess what? I
didn't get the part.

The next day, I got called in to audition for the same show,
even the same episode, but for a different character. This role
was much smaller and, much like my other roles, didn't require
much acting. I got that one! Yippee!

I showed up to work and realized that my part was in the
same episode as the role of Topanga. This was pretty cool,

because I got to see how the girl who got the job acted the part out. They obviously liked her, so maybe I could learn something from her.

First of all, this girl was incredibly sweet. She was also very talented. The role was meant for someone who could talk very slowly and still be funny. She seemed to know how to do that. I watched her work with our director the whole first day. Even though I had been in acting classes before, this was like my first real lesson. It changed my life.

I remember David Trainer, our exceptionally gifted director for the first two seasons, giving her notes on how to improve her performance. She seemed to have trouble there. He'd give her a note telling her to change something, and she'd do it the exact same way again. I felt like a little kid in a classroom; I wanted to raise my hand and say, "Can I try?" Even at twelve, I knew that was unprofessional, so I kept my mouth shut.

On set the next day, she wasn't there. They had let her go, and the executive producer, Michael Jacobs, needed to find a new girl to play Topanga. To this day, I don't know why Michael gave me another opportunity to audition for Topanga, although I suspect it was because it was easier than having to do a whole new casting call, but he did. It was down to me and another girl, Marla Sokoloff, who was also doing a guest spot on the episode.

I knew this was my chance to show everyone how much I had learned about acting since they saw me last. I had to shine. *I had to be Topanga.*

Marla went in first. When she came out of her audition, the casting director was gushing over her. "Please, give me every possible number where I can find you tonight in case we need to get hold of you," is what the casting director said to Marla's mom. I felt like I was already at a disadvantage.

I went in for my audition. When I was done, the casting director said, "Thanks, Danielle." That was it. Just "Thanks, Danielle." No begging for phone numbers. *Nada*.

My mom and I walked to the car, and I started sobbing. I told her there was no way I got the part and I wanted it so badly. She was very comforting and tried to remind me that we didn't know anything for sure yet.

What we did know for sure was that we needed to call my dad. He was expecting us home hours earlier and was anxious to hear how my second day on the job had gone. This was 1993 and long before the convenience of small cell phones you could carry around in your pocket or purse. But my mom had a pager, which is hilarious to me now, because if someone has a pager today, I automatically assume they deal drugs. My mom might drive seventy miles per hour in a sixty-five-mph zone, and one time she did call a man a "jerk head" for honking at her, but she has never sold drugs.

She also had a "car phone." When I asked my mom to describe the details of the phone for me so I could include them in this story, she said, "It was a phone that never had good service, cost a million dollars per minute to use, and was massive."

Basically, she had Zack Morris's phone from *Saved by the Bell*.

My dad had been paging my mom for the last few hours, wondering where we were. The minute we were in the car, we called him.

My mom was driving and wanted to be safe, so she handed me the phone, and I started to tell my dad about the events of the day. I don't remember the exact words of the conversation, but I know he asked me to repeat myself several times. Partly because of the bad car-phone service and partly because I hadn't stopped crying.

And then it happened. My dad got another call and put me on hold. He came back and said, "Some woman named Sally Stiner just called and said that you should come back to work tomorrow as Topanga? What does that mean?"

I started screaming. Sally Stiner was the casting director. I started bouncing up and down—seat belt on, of course, safety first—and yelled, "I got Topanga!" My mom started screaming, and my poor dad still had no idea what was going on. I finally calmed down and told him the whole story.

The next day, I went back to work with my new role. I worked hard all day and thought I was nailing it. And then we had a run-through.

A run-through is exactly what it sounds like. You "run through" the episode of the show you've been rehearsing for the last couple of days. It's basically a full performance of that week's show for all the producers, writers, and network executives. It gives everyone a chance to see what's really working in the episode and where changes need to be made. When the run-through is complete, all the actors sit together in front of all the writers and get notes on what was good and what, well, wasn't so good.

I was incredibly nervous during my first run-through as Topanga. I knew Michael had high expectations for all his actors, and I wasn't going to be any different. But I felt pretty darn good about how I had performed. How bad could it be, really?

On *BMW*, we did our notes session in the Matthews family's living room. I can remember exactly where I was sitting when Michael started off the notes session with me. "Danielle," he said, "there were a few things you did really well today, but overall, you are way off from where I want you to be. I have so many notes for you that I'm not going to make everyone else sit here while I give them to you. We'll be here all night. I'll speak with you privately after we're done here."

Then I had to sit for what felt like hours, listening to everyone else get minor notes about small adjustments they needed to make with their performances. I only had this job because they had already fired the first girl. Was I going to get fired? Marla was still on set and playing the same role she'd had from the beginning. They could easily decide that they had made a mistake and give the role of Topanga to her. As quickly as the opportunity came to me, it could be taken away just as fast. I was a ball of nervous energy, and it was a miracle that I didn't pee my pants while sitting there.

When the notes session was over, Michael pulled my mom and me into the Matthews family's kitchen. We sat down and went over every single line I had in the script. Michael told me exactly what he wanted from me. It was surprisingly different from what I had been doing, but I knew I could handle it. Michael ended the conversation by telling me that I had one more day to get this right . . . and if I didn't, they'd have to recast the role. I wanted to cry.

My mom and I went home and got right to work on the script. My mom read my lines with me and gave me notes on what Michael wanted. We did this until four A.M., when my mom and I eventually passed out. When we woke up, my mom said, "You can do this, Danielle." I wasn't quite as confident.

We drove to the set, and I worked all day with the director. He seemed pleased with the adjustments I had made, but all I really cared about was getting positive feedback from Michael. Unfortunately, I had to wait all day for another run-through to see if my changes were worthy of that.

The run-through came and went, and once again, I felt pretty good about what I had done. This time, however, I was painfully aware that I had felt the same way the day before, when I was told my whole performance needed to change if I wanted to keep my job.

Michael started the notes session off with me again. My heart stopped beating regularly, and my palms got sweaty. "Danielle, yesterday I gave you an enormous amount of notes. I did that because I believed you were capable of handling them," he said in front of all the writers and producers and my fellow actors. Then he stood up. I panicked. Was he going to fire me, slam his script on the ground, and storm out of there? "However, with your performance today, you exceeded my expectations," he concluded. He started clapping, and all the writers stood up and clapped next to him. Michael wasn't going to fire me. He believed in me. He gave me a freaking standing ovation.

To this day, I've never felt such a rush of emotion. I was so happy I wanted to jump for joy. I had been included in this family of talented people and had earned the right to be there with my hard work and the hard work of my mom, who not only believed in me but helped me and encouraged me.

As you know, Topanga did become a recurring character for seasons one and two and eventually became a series regular, present in every episode. When people ask me what my favorite episode of *BMW* is, my answer is always "Cory's Alternative Friends," because it was such a roller coaster of emotion for me and it changed the course of my whole life. It was also the episode when I had my first on-screen kiss and my first real-life kiss.

After you've had the benefits of being a series regular on a sitcom for seven years, you have a new sort of auditioning freedom. You have some money in the bank, and you start thinking, *Maybe I don't have to go on that audition to play the sexy high*

school dropout who tragically, yet comically, loses an eye while playing beer pong with her controlling but gorgeous boyfriend. Or the
athlete's foot commercial. Or the fourth-season reality show. Maybe,
just maybe, I'm too good for that crap now.

I confess that when I finished *Boy Meets World*, this was my
frame of mind. I would like to say that I insisted on only the
most top-notch, crème-de-la-crème roles, but I didn't want to be
too cocky. Instead, I said simply that I didn't want to audition
for any roles in horror movies or soap operas. See? I'm open-
minded!

For the record, I only dislike horror movies because I *hate*
being scared. I do not get the appeal. I once went to Halloween
Horror Nights at Universal Studios with a guy I was dating. I'm
sure he thought that this was going to be a romantic night as
he protected me from all the scary ghouls and goblins. We were
standing in a dark room with neon-green polka dots when a
man wearing a black suit with neon-green polka dots jumped
out of the wall at me. I screamed, punched him in the face, and
then cried for two hours. My date took me home and never
called me again. I was so good at dating.

As for soap operas, my mom used to watch them when I was
a kid, and even then, I felt bad for the talented actors stuck working with that *writing*! My God, the writing. I will say, though,
that my love of the British accent started with Finola Hughes,
who played Anna Devane on *General Hospital*. I used to sit in
front of the mirror and practice my accent into my microphone/

hairbrush. (I also used that same microphone brush to act out my future appearance on *Oprah*, where I would obviously discuss my insanely perfect marriage to Jordan Knight of New Kids on the Block, but that's a story for another time.)

Unfortunately, Hollywood wasn't as ready to begin its love affair with me as I was with them. After spending several years being too good for these types of roles and not once working, I decided it might be time to expand my horizons. Perhaps I could learn to love being scared; I did have an above-average "I'm frightened" face, usually elicited when I spilled chili dip down my white silk blouse at Thanksgiving. And perhaps *General Hospital* deserves the Pulitzer Prize for soap-opera writing. So in a fit of (forced) enthusiasm, I called up my agent and said "Bring. It. On."

It didn't take him long to find some choice projects, and I got a call a few days later. "Danielle, we have two auditions for you on the same day next week. The first is for the horror movie *Cabin Fever*, and the second is for *The Bold and the Beautiful!*" Not my dream gigs, certainly, but after a few years of fruitless auditions, I would take what I could get. I mustered all of my phony enthusiasm and said, "Great!" Within minutes, I'd printed off the sides—industry-speak for pages of the script you'll be reading during the audition—and started scanning.

At first, I was pleasantly surprised by the *Cabin Fever* scene. It was a horror movie about a group of kids who go camping for a weekend and somehow contract a flesh-eating virus. In the scene I was sent, I didn't have to do any ridiculous screaming, I didn't have any long, dramatic monologues, and I didn't die a horrible death. In fact, I didn't do much of anything. *Why'd they pick this scene?* I wondered to myself.

I read to the end and noticed that at the end, there were three-quarters of a page of stage directions. For anyone who hasn't seen a script, these are little notes that tell the reader what is going on in between the lines of dialogue. Things like "Karen puts her glass down and walks toward the door. Michael enters."

Usually during an audition, you don't act these things out, you just carry on with your dialogue. So at the very end of my *Cabin Fever* scene, I quickly scanned the stage directions and got on with memorizing my lines.

Next, I perused my *The Bold and the Beautiful* sides. I would be playing Melinda, a devious, sexy housemaid. The character was carrying on a torturous love affair with her married boss, who was going through a trying time and couldn't seem to shake his depression. Mental illness was hot stuff, apparently. During this scene, my boss would be sleeping on the couch in a robe. This would frustrate me for some reason, and I'd react by pouring a giant glass of milk on his head.

Not having watched the show, I had no idea if this was a typical *Bold and the Beautiful* reaction, in a universe where evil twins wreak havoc on unsuspecting good twins and slapping your mother's face is an acceptable form of communication. But that's what it said: I was to pour milk on his head. The boss character would wake up, a little peeved, as you might imagine, and say, "What on earth are you doing?"

To which, I'd reply, passionately, "Can't you see I want to do more than pour cold milk on your head?"

To this day, I have zero idea what that means. For perhaps the same reason, I could not get myself to say it in a way that shows I have any acting talent at all. Every single time I read it—in my head, out loud, it didn't matter—I said, "Can't you see I want to do more than pour cold milk on your head?" like a live-action Stewie Griffin. I knew this line reading would have to change before I got into the room, but I put that off for later. It was one line. I could get past it.

When Wednesday, the day of my auditions, arrived, my first challenge was finding an outfit that said both "horror" and "sexy housemaid," without being, you know, heavy-handed. I decided on a cute top and jeans. I mean, I didn't want my outfit to over-shadow the amazing performance I was about to give, right?

I got to the *Cabin Fever* waiting room five minutes early and signed in. Shortly after I got there, I realized the audition was a producer's callback. There were at least five people in the room, plus a camera. I was surprised, but it was nothing I couldn't han-dle. I started the scene, finished my two-ish pages of dialogue, and said thank you when I was done. Feeling pretty good about the way it went, I had turned toward the door to let myself out when I heard, "Oh, no. I'm sorry, but we need you to finish the scene."

I turned around.

"I did finish the scene. In the sides I have, the dialogue ends after my last line." Maybe I was given the wrong sides? It wouldn't be the first time that had happened, so it was entirely possible that things had changed since I was sent the script.

"Yeah," the director said. "There isn't any more dialogue, but we need you to act out the stage directions at the end."

Oh no.

"OK," I said. "May I just have a minute, please?" I turned around and quickly read those directions I'd briefly scanned the week before. Suddenly, words I hadn't noticed before were jumping out at me:

Port-a-potty.

Peeing.

Flesh.

Melting flesh.

And, of course, *screaming.*

You have got to be kidding me.

I turned back around. "You want me to *act out* going to the bathroom in a port-a-potty?" I asked them.

"Yes! Yes, we do."

At this point, I decided that I couldn't care less if I got this part. I just wanted to get out of that room without losing all of my dignity. And yet I was a professional. I mimed the scene as follows: *Oh, hey, a port-a-potty. Great. I have to go really bad.* I entered, closed the fake door behind me, and did the hovercraft (if you're a woman, you know what this is; if you're a man, have a woman explain it to you).

Now, here's where it got tricky. How do you mime going to the bathroom? Whatever. I reminded myself that I really didn't want this job anyway, but my Type A personality was raging inside my head. To myself, I thought I must have looked incredibly stupid. Not because I was squatting in thin air but because the director couldn't know whether I'd started going or not.

I shook that thought, continued pretending (i.e., hovering and looking bored), looked down, made a concerned expression—*What's this?*—and gasped.

Now for my shining moment of glory. I had to imagine—and *act out* in front of a room full of people—what it would be like to discover *melting flesh* (just another day at the office), scream my head off, and try to get out of the invisible port-a-potty, miming motions of being trapped. In the back of my head, I already couldn't wait to tell my mom about this. I exited the port-a-potty in terror (did I forget to flush the fake toilet?) left the stage, and scene.

I have never run out of a room so fast in my life.

Afterward, as you might imagine, I spent a lot of time questioning my career choice and deciding whether I should walk into Marie Callender's and apply for a waitressing position or head to my next audition. I figured there was no way the *Bold and the Beautiful* audition could be as humiliating as what I'd just experienced, so off I went.

You'd think I would have learned by then.

When I got to the next waiting room and signed in, not a single other soul was there. A few minutes went by, and I started getting nervous. Did I have the right day? Ten more minutes passed, and I was still the only person in the waiting room. Finally, it occurred to me what was happening. They'd already chosen me for the role! *Look, they're not even auditioning any other girls! Ha.* I was so proud of myself.

However, after twenty-five more minutes passed, my mental state went from confused, to elated, to pissed. I couldn't wait for them to offer me this role, just so I could turn it down on principle! How dare they make me wait for close to an hour without even coming out to check on me. Why did casting directors think they were the only ones who had lives? That was it. I was finally going to take a stand for actors everywhere and just leave!

Except I didn't. Fifteen minutes later, I was still fuming in the waiting room when the casting director finally appeared and said those seven magic words: "All right, I'm ready for you now." And "Sorry for the wait."

Ready for me *now*? Was she serious? I decided to give her a piece of my mind, but what came out was something like "Oh, it's no problem. Thanks for seeing me." I like to think there was a note of sarcasm in my voice but probably not. I needed this audition.

We got into the room, and she turned on the camera. "Do you have any questions for me?" she asked.

"No, I'm good to go."

"OK," she said. "I'm going to have you state your name, age, height, and weight." Age and weight, huh? That was a new one, but all right. "Then," she continued, "I'm going to need you to hold your arms out to the side and turn three hundred sixty degrees, very slowly, while I pan the camera up and down your body." Ah, the entertainment industry. Where talent and ability are less important than height and weight. I knew I should have gone to Marie Callender's!

We started the scene. Everything was going well until it was time to pour the milk on homeboy's head. Out of my mouth came "Can't you see I want to do more than pour cold milk on your head?"

The casting director stopped me. "Can we do the scene again, and this time say the milk line like you have been in love with him for years, and you just want him to acknowledge he loves you, too?"

"Oh, yeah, sure," I said. "That's no problem. I've been doing this line different ways all week. *Can't you see I want to do more than pour cold milk on your head?*"

She stopped me again; one more time.

"Can't you see I want to do more than pour cold milk on your head?"

Every time, I said it the exact same way. It was like I'd been possessed and a robot had taken over my brain. I could not say it any other way. It was *horrible*. I knew it was horrible, she knew it was horrible, and the camera knew it was horrible. The next time she stopped me, I finally made up my mind.

"Listen," I said. "I understand this may not be the line reading you're looking for, but it is the choice I've made for the character, and I'm not willing to budge on it." That's called dramatic integrity, folks. She looked at me incredulously and thanked me for my time.

It will not surprise you, but I was not offered either role. However, I am pleased to say that since that day, I have never auditioned for another horror movie or soap opera. And you know why? Because I may not be perfect, but we are all too good for that crap.

CHAPTER 2

WALK MUCH?

Before we take our relationship any further, I have something important to tell you. Hello, my name is Danielle Fishel, and I am a total klutz. Not just the fall-in-high-heels normal type of klutzes we all know. I mean a serious fall-down-out-of-nowhere, embarrass-the-hell-out-of-friends-and-family type of klutz. If there is something to trip on, I will trip on it. Frankly, if there is nothing to trip on, I will trip anyway. Or spill my drink. Or put my foot in my mouth within five minutes of meeting someone.

Apparently, this is something I've done my whole life. When my mom recounts stories of what I was like as a child, I'm often ridiculously embarrassed. People who have children know that sometimes, actually, 99.99 percent of the time, you have no control over what comes out of your child's mouth. Thanks to Bill Cosby, those of us without children know that *Kids Say the*

Darndest Things. I fit that description if by *darndest* Mr. Cosby meant rudest.

When I was three years old, my mom took me to McDonald's. We were sitting in a little booth in the middle of the restaurant. Sitting next to us was a very portly person who had quite a bit of food: multiple orders of fries, a few burgers, and some chicken nuggets. I was enthralled.

One of the most confusing things to me about children is how hard it is to get them to eat. I've been around a good number of kids, and every single time, I've had to force them to stop playing and shove some food down their gullets. Who doesn't finish a peanut butter and jelly sandwich? Who leaves fries on a plate? Who takes three bites of dinner and asks to be excused so they can go play in the dirt? I'm sure child Danielle did, but adult Danielle would love to sit down to a meal of chicken nuggets and eat them all.

Child Danielle couldn't take her eyes off the person who was gobbling food down like it was a last meal. Crap, maybe it *was* a last meal! I had no way of knowing what was going on in that person's life. Who am I to judge the eating habits of a person enjoying a meal in McDonald's? I was there, too. I should have kept my prying eyes to myself and kept my loud mouth shut. I should have, but I didn't. Suddenly, and loudly, I exclaimed, "Ugh, Mommy, look! Why is that man eating like a *pig*?" I still had a fry in my own hand when my mom apologized to the *woman* I had so crudely insulted and yanked me out of that McDonald's before I even had time to protest.

As I got older, I learned not to be so judgmental or, at the very least, to keep my judgments to myself. Right around the same time as I learned to think about the feelings of others and not speak every time a thought entered my head, I came down with a case of the klutzes.

I could spin this differently. I could tell you that I've always been fearless when it comes to athletics. I could tell you that I was a bit of a tomboy who regularly beat boys at sports when I was a child. I could tell you that I can throw a perfect spiral with a football and once had dreams of being a quarterback on a football team. But this isn't that story. This is the story of how I fell off a freaking Big Wheel.

Not my actual Big Wheel.

I grew up in Yorba Linda, California. It is a small suburb of Orange County and was a fantastic place to grow up in the 1980s. We lived on a small cul-de-sac, and there were several kids my age who became my best friends. We all went to the same elementary school and played at one another's houses. Our moms became friends, and we frequently spent weekends having sleepovers. Jessica was my bestest best friend, and she lived one small street away from me. We lived so close that my mom could stand outside our house and watch me travel the short distance to and from Jessica's house.

One evening, just before dinner, I left Jessica's house on my Big Wheel. I had lead feet and could really make that thing go. Not sure what the horsepower is on a Big Wheel, but I think it must be at least five hundred. The only problem with the Big Wheel was that sometimes, when you pedaled really fast, the wheels stopped spinning but your feet kept moving. It was incredibly irritating. Just when you got going, the wheels would stop, and your feet would be uselessly pedaling. That's exactly what happened on that fateful day that permanently scarred my face. Damn you, Big Wheel!

Naturally, when you're young, everything looks bigger. The street that connected Jessica's house to my house had a small curve, but when I was five, this curve seemed fit for a NASCAR race. I was supposed to be home before dinner, and, as usual, Jessica and I had played a few minutes longer than we should have, so I was in a hurry to get home. I hopped onto my trusty five-hundred-hp Big Wheel and took off.

I was on the asphalt and riding along the left side of the road, near the curb. But then I hit a roadblock. A car was parked in front of a home along my path. I could have driven on the curb, but the road was curving away from my house in that direction, and there wasn't a "curb exit" before my own home. Had I taken the curb, I would have ended up on a busier street that was strictly forbidden for playing and riding Big Wheels. I had no choice. I had to ride my Big Wheel in the middle of the street.

I expertly managed my Big Wheel around the parked car and was in the middle of the road. And then I heard it. The sound of an oncoming car. I was merely inches off the ground in a brightly colored Big Wheel, and I was going to get hit by a car. I pedaled my little legs as fast as I could and spun the handles of my Big Wheel toward the curb. My wheels stopped. My feet kept moving. *Not now, Big Wheel!* But it was too late. I could see the wheels of the car rapidly coming toward me, and I had to make a quick decision. Panic or save myself? I chose to save myself by hurling my body off the Big Wheel and onto the asphalt. The Big Wheel tipped over, and we were both sliding across the pebbly, black, filthy asphalt. My face broke my fall. I was bleeding, and barely any skin remained on my face.

Sure, this experience was tragic for me at the time, but let's be honest here. Who "falls off" a Big Wheel? How does one

This was after my face had healed somewhat.
Also, sweet shirt and bow I have there, huh?

manage to do that? How does one manage to fall off something that barely sits off the ground? And if we want to talk reality, that car was probably going less than ten miles per hour. It was also on the opposite side of the road from me, because that's how we drive in America. I was never in any real danger, except for the danger I put myself in by being born with a serious case of the klutzes.

Over the next few weeks, my face scabbed over and I looked horrendous. I didn't want scabs on my face—who does? I had one scab in particular that really ticked me off. It was one of the smaller scabs, but it was located directly under my right nostril. To me, it looked as if a brown booger was constantly hanging out of my nose, and I wanted it gone. So I would pick at it. Naturally, it would come back. I'd pick at it again. Of course, it would come back, so I'd pick it yet again. This went on despite my mother begging me to stop because it would scar. I didn't care.

Sure enough, my whole face healed pretty well, except for that one little spot under my nose. It scarred, all right. It scarred in a way that looks like I have snot running out of my nose and down toward my upper lip. Every makeup artist who has ever put makeup on me has delicately dabbed that spot on my face with a makeup sponge at least five times before I realize what's going on.

"Oh, sorry," I say. "That's actually not snot. It's a scar. It's my snot scar."

And then I remember my faulty Big Wheel and how it left me for dead in my time of need.

The Big Wheel incident is the first memory I have of being klutzy, but it didn't stop there (there *is* an entire chapter here on the subject, friends).

I'm pleased to introduce to you some of the most awkward years in anyone's life: high school.

The *Boy Meets World* filming schedule made it impossible for me to attend my regular high school full-time, but being as normal as possible—despite having one of the most unusual jobs ever—has always been important to my parents and me, so I went to "real" school as often as I could.

I enjoyed my classes on the *BMW* set, but I *loved* real school. There were so many more boys to look at, and I had made some really good friends. I liked sitting at the same lunch table every day, hearing my friends talk about the guys they liked or the classes they hated. Being at real school was also the only way I would ever know exactly what had gone on in the latest episode of *Beverly Hills 90210*, because my mom thought it was "too mature" for me to watch. I had to hear about the adventures and sexual escapades of Brandon, Kelly, Dylan, and Brenda from my friends, who clearly had cooler parents than I did. I mean, I was twelve! Did they think I was some kind of child or something? The nerve!

So, it's pretty obvious why *I* loved being at my real school as much as possible, but most child actors choose to do all of their schooling on set for a few reasons. First, it can be distracting to other students when another student is gone for long periods of time shooting a movie or a TV show, and then he or she just reappears halfway through the year. It's even annoying and distracting for the teachers. During one particularly horrible year of junior high school, I had a mean, tiny, angry jerk face of a teacher. He hated me and called me Princess. I'd come back to school after being gone for three weeks filming episodes of *BMW*, and he'd say, "Oh, welcome back, Princess," in the most condescending way. He almost always followed it up with "Look everyone! Princess decided to come back and join us. Aren't we lucky?" I used to have dreams of stepping on his head and crushing him beneath the Converse shoes I wore every single day. I also wore a flannel around my waist every day because it was the '90s, and "grunge" was the look. A baby T, flannel around my waist, and Converse were as far as my good sense/mother would let me take grunge. I was like ten percent committed to the trend.

Second, junior high and high school can be cruel no matter who you are. All those hormones, insecurities, and never having a clue if you actually fit in with your peers make for some pretty lousy humans wandering around their campus like they own the joint. Sometimes child actors are easy targets, because they aren't there all the time, and it can be easy to make fun of the commercials, TV shows, or movies they've done. From ten to twelve years old, I did a few Mattel commercials where I played the live-action Skipper. She was Barbie's younger, not nearly as cool, sister. "Skipper" became my nickname on day one of sixth grade, and outside of my circle of friends, I don't think anyone knew my real name. Luckily for me, there are a lot worse nicknames ("Fish Lips" was another contender for me, but that one didn't stick) so "Skipper" didn't bother me. I kind of liked it.

Finally, coming and going from regular school to set school can be extremely difficult. As a minor in California, your time on set is limited to ten and a half hours a day. About three to four hours of that time must be spent doing schoolwork each day. Obviously, regular school hours are quite a bit longer, so the education on set is usually done at a faster pace, and one needs to be incredibly focused. If you're getting half of your education on set and the other half at your regular school, that means you need to be caught up to precisely the same lessons as the rest of your peers when you do attend regular classes. That means that you need to be getting your lesson plans from the regular school you are attending, which isn't always easy. Teachers don't *have* to have their entire year's lesson plans mapped out at the beginning of the year. As a matter of fact, most of them don't. They also don't *have* to be understanding or supportive of your career choice at age ten. Some teachers and schools are incredible at being organized and doing everything they can to help out a child in that position. Some of them aren't. Either way, that was a challenge I wanted to take on, because even though I loved being on the *BMW* set, I wanted to be at school every chance I had.

I went to almost every high school football game and attended almost every school dance. I had to miss one dance because I got caught smoking at sixteen and my parents, rightfully, grounded me. (Man, my parents really didn't miss a beat. I'm exhausted just thinking about how diligent they were.) I had a lot of wonderful friends and was completely boy-crazy. Honestly, I couldn't have cared less about learning. Learning *shmearning*. Who could even think of talking about U.S. history when winter formal was coming up and I needed a dress? Who cared about math when that beautiful senior boy had just passed me a note in the hallway? Why did I need English when I speaked good already?

My freshman year, I couldn't have been more excited to go to winter formal. My mom offered to take me shopping for a dress at our local mall—the Topanga Mall. No, seriously. Our local mall was called the Topanga Mall because it was on Topanga Boulevard. But instead of going to the Topanga Mall for a dress, my mom and I decided to take a trip to super-fancy Rodeo Drive after work on *BMW* one day. Even though we didn't live too far from Beverly Hills, we had never been there. We thought it would be fun to feel like *Pretty Woman* for a day. Not the pretty woman with pleather thigh-high boots, her tummy exposed in something that vaguely resembled a dress, and a horrible blond wig in a bob cut. We wanted to feel like the fancy pretty woman who wore a big floppy hat and white gloves and made those stupid, rude clerks feel like losers. Well, we didn't really want to wear hats or gloves, and we certainly didn't want to make anyone feel bad . . . You know what? I don't think this reference is working. We just thought it would be fun to window-shop at a fancy place.

While we were there, we walked into Jessica McClintock. This was the '90s, and Jessica McClintock prom dresses were *everything*. All of the dresses were super-fancy and shiny and had fake gems all over them. Obviously, fake gems made me feel dizzy with excitement, and I had never seen dresses more beautiful. I was in love. I found a floor-length emerald-green dress on the sale rack and tried it on. It had a slit up one leg and fake gems all over the spaghetti straps. I felt like royalty, and I never wanted to take it off. I begged my mom to buy me this, at the time, ridiculously expensive $110 sale-rack dress, and she did. Screw *90210*, my mom *was* cool!

A couple of days later, we went shopping at the Topanga Mall for shoes to go with my luxurious gown. My mom spotted the most amazing high heels. They were black satin and had tons of thin straps that crisscrossed all over the tops of my feet. They even had ankle straps. I *loved* ankle straps!

The night of my first-ever high school dance arrived, and my date looked so handsome at the bottom of the staircase in his suit. My dress fit me like a glove, my shoes were outrageously gorgeous, my hair was curled perfectly by my mom, and my makeup was flawless. My mom had invited our family over to take pictures of this momentous occasion in a girl's life. Everyone was waiting with bated breath for me to make my grand entrance (well, in my mind, they were waiting with bated breath, so let's roll with that). Cameras were out and pointed at the top of the stairs where I would be making my reveal. I came out from around the corner of the stairs and posed. I put on my best Madonna "Vogue" impression, arms in the air, hands turned out, with my face tilted slightly to the left and gently skyward. I was really milking this moment.

Never once did I look down. I did, however, make a different but equally glamorous pose for every step. I knew that house well. I knew those stairs well. I didn't need to look where I was going. About halfway down the stairs, I mentally prepared my next pose while I gently lifted my left foot to step down. In a flash, I felt my foot slip out my from under me. Internally, I panicked that the conservative yet sexy slit in my dress was going to rip, my heels were going to break, and this was going to be my first and last high school dance. In four-inch heels, I had stepped on a magazine that someone (fine—it was me) had left on the stairs, and I was going down. Hard. And fast. Did I mention hard? I hit every single step with an enormous thud. It sounded

One of my famous stair poses.

like an elephant had slipped on a banana peel. My curled hair was wrapped around my neck and stuck in my lip gloss. My legs were nearly in split position.

When I landed on the hard floor at the bottom of the staircase, there was silence. One second of silence followed immediately by the roaring laughter of ten family members and my date. I picked myself up off the floor and tried to regain my composure. My mom was bent over holding her stomach from laughing so hard. I hoped her stomach hurt as much as my body did. My dress was unharmed, my shoes were still perfection, and my date still wanted to go out in public with me. I laughed about my clumsiness with my family to rid myself of my humiliation, and my date and I took some quick photos. We then went to the dance, where, despite my soreness, I managed to tear that dance floor up, in my humble opinion.

Years later, I was invited to a Halloween party at a gigantic house in Los Angeles. I've never been a big fan of Halloween, because I don't consider myself to be a super-creative person. Coming up with a Halloween costume that is topical, funny, smart, and, for women, somehow ends up being "sexy" is a lot of pressure. I know people who start planning their Halloween costumes in May! I'd rather put a mask on and pass out candy to children while my dogs bark furiously at them and threaten to bite their tiny fingers off. *That* is a good time.

For some reason, I agreed to go to this particular Halloween party. Because I felt pressure to be creative, I allowed myself

If anyone knows what this costume is, please let me know.

ample time to shop and went out to pick the perfect costume on October 31. What? You're telling me *that's* the date of Halloween? Hmmm. Weird. Even with *all that time* to shop, there were hardly any good costumes left for some reason! I ended up picking an off-the-shoulder milkmaid costume.

I think that's what it was. I'm honestly not sure what I was supposed to be, and, sadly, I wasn't any more sure as I was putting the stupid thing on years ago. *Oh, well,* I thought at the time, *at least I'm comfortable.* (No, I wasn't even remotely comfortable.)

Immediately upon arriving, my friends decided that we needed to experience the haunted house that had been built in the guesthouse on the property. Because I don't like being scared, I mildly protested but ended up agreeing. I didn't want to be the fuddy-duddy who ruined everyone else's good time. (I mean, I'm already a Halloween fuddy-duddy because I hate wearing costumes, and I'm a fuddy-duddy because I use the term *fuddy-duddy*.)

The walk to the guesthouse/haunted house was a bit treacherous, especially for someone like me who rarely takes more than two steps without tripping. The property was absolutely gorgeous and had winding stone paths that led people to all the different areas of the perfectly landscaped yard. The particular path that we were walking along was downhill. Because I'm incredibly tall at five feet one inch, I was wearing five-inch heels that had a platform of an inch and a half and straps that tied up around my ankles. They weren't comfortable, and walking on flat ground was hard enough. Walking downhill in them on uneven stone was just plain stupid.

There were people everywhere. I knew there were super-famous people surrounding me on all sides, but I rarely recognize people. I don't know why or how that's possible, but I'm not sure I would recognize most famous people even if they slapped me in the face—which has never happened, surprisingly. My friends, the horde of famous guests, and I were all walking gingerly down the winding path. Out of nowhere, I was on my face. I had stumbled over a portion of uneven stone and my ridiculous shoes had decided to fling me to the ground rather than break my ankle. Thanks, ridiculous shoes. Anyway, I was facedown on the stone, which up close was actually kind of broken. There were small stones and dirt and generally really sharp edges everywhere. My hands were cut up in a thousand places, and using my sleuthlike investigation skills, I deciphered that my lip was bleeding because I could taste blood. Oh, and it hurt like hell. Wasn't I so smart to have figured that out with only those two minor and insignificant clues? I may be a klutz, but gosh darn it, I are a genius.

While I was splayed out on the ground in a surprisingly ladylike way, I tried to decide if I should cover my face with my hair and run out of the party as fast as I could or just pray for an immediate death. My friends kept asking if I was OK and were trying to help me stand up while also not falling over themselves. I said, "I'm fine. Just let me sit here for a second." What I was thinking was *I'm fine, just let the earth open up underneath me and swallow me whole so I don't have to stand up and make eye contact with another soul for as long as I live.* I could hear jerky people laughing at me. (Just kidding—I laugh every time someone falls, and that doesn't make *me* a jerk. It does? Oh.)

Suddenly, I was scooped up in someone's arms and hoisted into the air. Yes! My prayers had been answered, and I could hope that a fiery death was imminent, because that sounded so sweet right then. I looked at my captor and realized something horrific. He was terrifyingly handsome. Like incredibly, ruggedly, mind-bogglingly handsome. And he looked so familiar.

He said, "Oh, my God. Are you OK? That was a pretty bad fall."

Laughing it off, I said, "Haha, yeah, it was. I guess. But I'm fine. Totally fine. Actually, can you put me down, please?"

He looked at my knee, which I was also seeing for the first time. My fishnet panty hose were torn at both knees, and blood was running all the way down my left leg. My first thought was something like *Please don't bleed on this handsome man, Danielle,* and my next thought was, *Holy moly, this man is Ben Affleck. This handsome giant is Ben freaking Affleck, and you might bleed on him.* He put me down and told me to be careful. And just like that, he was gone. As quickly as he had come to rescue me, not laugh at me (which I totally would have done if he had fallen), he was gone.

I never met Mr. Affleck again. He probably wouldn't remember me (please, oh please, tell me he doesn't remember me), and that's fine. I will forever remember him as the handsome man who rescued me at a party.

I skipped the haunted house and went inside the party. I took my stupid fishnets off and cleaned up my bloody knee. I ate a few delicious chocolate-covered strawberries and took this now infamous photo.

See that girl I'm with in the Poison Ivy costume? That's one of my best friends, also named Danielle. She saw this picture, noticed the huge chunk of strawberry in my teeth, and laughed so hard she cried. She printed it out, and to this day, it is framed and on display in her home.

<u>TAKEAWAY TIPS</u>

- Ben Affleck is an infinitely better human being than I am.
- My friend Danielle is an infinitely worse human being than Ben Affleck.

CHAPTER 3

AS SEEN ON TV

Want to hear something that is crazy to me? I've been known as the character Topanga for twice as long as I've been known as just Danielle. For two-thirds of my life, I've been Danielle but also Topanga. That's more than twenty years of living with an alter ego whom I couldn't be more proud to be associated with. Topanga is smart, caring, devoted, funny, and a feminist. Playing Topanga in the early years of *Boy Meets World* is still, by far, the most fun I've ever had on a job. She was different from any other TV character and completely authentic. She was a little wacky, totally secure, and absolutely not fazed by what other people thought about her. I think she is a great role model for girls, and truthfully, she has always been a great role model for me.

Somewhere during the seven years we filmed *BMW*, Topanga and I became more and more similar. It became hard to know what was definitively her and what was definitively me. As I said, I think Topanga rocks, so this was not a bad thing. It was only a bad thing when other people had a hard time decipher-ing who was who. That may sound silly, because most people understand that actors play characters on TV and they aren't *actually* those characters in real life, but you might be surprised how many people forget that fact when an actor is standing in front of their face.

During the fourth season of *BMW*, we filmed a two-part epi-sode called "A Long Walk to Pittsburgh." In part one, Topanga is forced to move to Pittsburgh with her parents. In case you aren't a fan of the show, what the heck are you doing with your life? Just kidding. No, I'm not. Anyway, if you aren't familiar with the show, it's important for you to know that Topanga was deeply and madly in love with Cory. Cory was equally deeply and madly in love with Topanga, so this move from Philadel-phia to Pittsburgh was not going to be easy on them. They had never been apart. How were they going to make it? It was a very emotional episode for our fans (or, as I call them, friends we haven't met who have incredible taste), and many people were distraught thinking about what this move meant for our charac-ters and their relationship.

During part two of the episode, Topanga shows up at Cory's door, soaking wet after having traveled in the rain all the way back to Philly for Cory, her true love. When we filmed the episode, we played part one for the studio audience who were there to watch us film part two. We had just filmed part one the week before, so obviously, it hadn't aired on TV yet. We needed the audience to know exactly what had happened in the first part in order to hear and see their natural reaction to part two. Because everyone loves a good surprise, the producers put up a huge black curtain to block the audience's view of what was happening on set in front of them. I had to sneak around behind the set to get behind the curtain so no one in the audience could see me. When Cory opened the door and Topanga was revealed, looking like a wet rat, having traveled hundreds of miles to get back to her man, the audience let out the most amazing gasp. Thanks to that black curtain, they had no idea Topanga would be standing there. The gasp was immediately followed by a huge round of applause, and you can hear every awesome second of it when you watch the episode.

Moments like that were never short of incredible, but our fans' love for Cory and Topanga also made for some awkward run-ins with people in public. A few months after we filmed "A Long Walk to Pittsburgh," the show aired on ABC. The following weekend, I was at Universal Studios with my then-boyfriend. We were sixteen and having a great time walking around, eating, and holding hands—just enjoying being totally infatuated with each other. At one point, I looked up and noticed another kid about our same age glaring at me. He was walking a few paces ahead of us and kept looking over his shoulder, giving me the stink-eye. I think the kids today call it "throwing shade," but I'm not cool enough to pull that off. I mentioned it to my boyfriend.

"Hey, that guy keeps giving us dirty looks. Do you know him?"

He replied, "Which one? Oh, that one? No. I don't know him. Just ignore him."

After about three totally awkward minutes of homie throwing me shade (yep, just doesn't feel right) and me feeling completely creeped out and confused, the guy spun on his heels right in front of us.

GUY: Hey. What's going on here?

BOYFRIEND: What's your problem, man? Why do you keep giving us dirty looks?

GUY: Um, well, helloooo? I know who *she* is, but I don't know what's going on here. Who are *you*?

ME: Whoa. This is my boyfriend, and we're just hanging out here today. Just like you are.

GUY: No! How could you? I just watched you come back for Cory in the rain!

ME: Oh. Well, that was for television. I'm not Topanga in real life, you know? My name is Danielle.

I have never seen a more confused look on a person's face in my life. He had no idea what I was talking about. TV? Characters? Actor? What's that? All he knew was that I was Topanga, Topanga was apparently a cheating tramp, and this loser I was with should have been Cory. Visibly upset, the guy stormed off.

Shortly after that, my boyfriend and I broke up. Not that shocking, considering that my longest relationship in high school lasted about six months. Unlike Topanga, I didn't have a Cory I knew I wanted to spend an eternity with. I could barely find a guy I wanted to share more than a burger with (shouts to Red Robin, my favorite restaurant for the majority of my life). Don't get me wrong. I was a little boy-crazy. I had crushes on new boys weekly and had visions of getting married someday and having a gaggle of kids. I just didn't want anything super-serious in high school. But I was super-serious about school dances. Man, did I love them.

I think every school has a dance where the whole point is that the girls are supposed to ask the guys instead of the other way around. It's actually a completely outdated concept and rather sexist to imply that the only time it's acceptable for a girl to ask a guy out is when it's the dance's shtick. Anyway, in my high school, that dance was called the vice-versa dance. Not going wasn't even an option, but I was boyfriend-less. I decided the absolute best person to bring would be Ben Savage.

Ben and I have always been close. I couldn't be more thankful for that, because I truly can't imagine a much worse work environment than being forced to act like soul mates with someone you actually despise. It probably wouldn't work. If Ben and I hadn't been such good friends, the Cory and Topanga relationship wouldn't have seemed real. It wouldn't have been believable to anyone, because that kind of intense chemistry can't be forced. I adored Ben, and no one made me laugh harder during the seven seasons we worked together. He was fun, willing to dance, and one of my best friends. He still is.

Ben came to my house to pick me up before the dance. He looked so handsome in his black suit, and we took a few pictures together. The plan for the evening was that we were going to go to the dance, immediately take the professionally staged photos, and then dance like fools for the rest of the night. I had my mini-purse with me, and inside was a lip gloss, some face powder, and a check to pay for the previously mentioned professional photos. The dance was a blast. Ben was the hit of the party and made quite a few friends. We both had an awesome time, and at the end of the night, we were some of the last people to leave. On our drive home, we talked about how hungry we were and decided to stop at Denny's for a late-night meal.

I don't remember what Ben ordered, but I can guarantee that I ordered eggs and toast, because that was, and still is, a staple of my diet. If it's on the menu, it's probably what I'm going to order if it's before five P.M. Or after nine P.M. Unless it's my birthday or my mom's birthday, because then we take each other out for pancakes. I guess you really don't care about what my restaurant orders are, huh? OK. Anyway, at the end of the meal, Ben grabbed at his pants pockets.

"Uh, Danielle? I left my wallet at your parents' house," he said.

"That's OK," I said as I reached for my mini-purse.

My mini-purse that didn't hold a wallet. My mini-purse that currently only had my license, a lip gloss, and a makeup compact in it.

"Ben. This is bad," I whispered. "I didn't bring any money, either! I just had the check for the professional pictures and some makeup!"

Ben and I sat in silence, staring into each other's eyes, over plates of scraps that barely passed as food.

After a few minutes, I said, "Is this gonna be the night that you and I have to wash Denny's dishes because we can't pay a twelve-dollar check?"

Ben thought that was reasonably funny, and his laugh broke the tension and slight panic we were both feeling. Then it hit me.

We went up to the front counter and asked the hostess if we could speak with the manager. Before she went to get him, she asked if she could take a picture with us, because she said she was a big fan. Ben and I looked at each other. "Sure," we said in unison as we both had flashes of how humiliating it was going to be to have to explain our situation to the manager.

The manager came out and asked what he could do for us.

I leaned in and very quietly said, "Hi. This is really embarrassing, but we both forgot our wallets at home. I live, like, five miles away. I promise that if you let us leave right now, we will come back in less than fifteen minutes to pay this bill. You can keep my mini-purse for collateral."

Yes, I offered my mini-purse, filled with nothing but makeup, as collateral to the Denny's manager. And it worked. The manager held on to my purse. Ben and I drove back to my house, grabbed our money, and went back and paid. We left our waitress a massive tip and thanked the entire staff profusely for trusting us. So that's how two famous and fairly wealthy teenagers found themselves broke at Denny's. Thank goodness TMZ didn't exist back then.

Not all stories about being recognized are as weird or embarrassing, but because I've been called Topanga for so long, sometimes I think I know what people are going to say before they say it. I'm not always right.

PERSON: Hi. Um, are you . . . are you . . . ?

ME: Yes, I am. Nice to meet you!

PERSON: Oh, my gosh! That's so cool. Where's your sister?

ME: Sister? Huh? I don't have a sister.

PERSON: Sorry, I mean your twin sister.

ME: Oh. You think I'm an Olsen twin, don't you?

PERSON: Yes?

ME: Sorry. Wrong person.

(totally awkward silence)

ME: OK, 'bye.

Then, sometimes, people don't know if you are the type of person who can be trusted.

PERSON: Excuse me, are you the girl who played Topanga?

ME: Yes, I am.

PERSON: No you're not!

ME: Yes, I am. Hi.

PERSON: No, you are not!!

ME: OK, fine. I'm not.

PERSON: Yes, you are!

ME: Yep. That's what I tried to tell you.

PERSON: No way. Are you really?

And occasionally, you meet people who have the absolute best intentions with what they're saying, but it just comes out wrong.

SCENARIO ONE

PERSON: Topanga?

ME: Yep. Hi.

PERSON: You're so much shorter in person. Did they put you on stilts for that show? Damn, you are short!

ME: Yes, I am. Have a good day.

SCENARIO TWO

PERSON: Are you the girl from *Boy Meets World*?

ME: Yeah. Hi. Nice to meet you.

PERSON: Jeez, you are so much smaller in person. On TV, you look so much fatter!

ME: Yay! OK, 'bye.

Generally, I love, truly love, when people come up and say hi to me. I am usually very nice and couldn't be more appreciative of those of you who have encouraged and supported my career for all these years. I am lucky to have you, and I am grateful that you even care to say hi, or take a picture, or shake my hand at all.

I've said no to pictures with people on two occasions, one was when I was leaving a funeral for someone very close to me. Aside from the fact that I had been sobbing for a few hours and had mascara running down my cheeks, I didn't feel the timing was appropriate, and it would have been disrespectful to the family. The other time I turned down taking a picture with someone was completely void of anything righteous and was strictly because I'm a vain jerk face. It was five thirty A.M., and I had just completed an hour-long boot-camp class that completely exhausted me. My face was bright red, I had zero makeup on, and my workout clothes looked like I had stolen them from a homeless woman around the corner. So, yeah. I said no that time, too. But, with that said, here's an open invitation. If you ever see me and you'd like a picture together, please come ask. I don't bite, and you will absolutely not be bothering me.

What does bother me, to the point of possibly biting someone's head off (wait, I thought I said I don't bite . . .), is when someone tries to take a picture of me without me knowing it. I am a nice person, but that doesn't mean I don't have a bitchy side. Trust me, I have one. If you ever want to see my bitchy side, see me out in public and try to take a picture of me without asking with your cell phone . . . preferably while I'm eating wings.

I don't know why people don't realize that everyone knows cell phones have cameras or why people don't think I can tell when they are awkwardly holding their phones in my direction, but they do. In my opinion, there are few things more rude than trying to take a picture of someone without his or her knowledge. Especially when they are eating!

A couple years ago I went to a restaurant/bar with my husband, Tim, and we ordered delicious, sauce-covered, disastrous-to-eat wings. I love wings. I love food. I love to not have people judging me while I'm eating food, because I am a human being and no one likes that. Just as I was fully investing myself in those deliciously messy wings and had sauce all over my face and fingers, the guy sitting in front of us held up his cell-phone camera. He was trying to take a picture of himself with my sauce-covered face behind him by using his phone's reverse camera view. I noticed it and quickly ducked behind Tim so I could use a napkin to clean the chicken sauce off my face, but that didn't deter the guy. He was waving his camera around like a madman, trying to find my face. And I could see this all happening twelve feet in front of me.

When I had successfully cleaned off my wing-sauce-stained face, I went over to him and said, "Would you like to take a picture? I'd rather we do it now so that you can stop trying to take my picture while I'm eating."

His response? "No. I didn't want to take your picture. I just wanted to know if it was you but didn't want to be rude and keep turning around to look."

Riiiiiiiiight. I don't know about you, but I call BS on that story.

Anyway, his friend chirped up and said, "Man, if you're offering, I definitely want a picture!"

Mr. Curious with the reverse-angle camera was the one who took it. He got up and left a few minutes later, probably planning to tell everyone he'd ever met that he met me once and I was a total witch. Sorry, dude, but who wants to have her picture taken looking like a slob with meat in her teeth and red sauce all over her face? Not a good look for anyone.

CHAPTER 4

SOMETIMES THEY WISH I WAS ADOPTED

My parents have had it pretty easy with me: I love and respect them and have managed to be a well-adjusted contributing member of society—most of the time. Not too shabby, right? But despite my good intentions, I can't seem to avoid being the occasional disgrace to their gene pool.

For example, take my skills behind the wheel. As is true for many sixteen-year-olds, when I first learned to drive, I left some room for improvement. I gripped the steering wheel too tightly, I drove too fast, I tailgated, and I hugged the right side of the road. Shortly after I started driving myself to work, I got into a terrible car accident on the freeway. It had been raining very heavily, and even though I was not speeding, I shouldn't have been in the fast lane. My beloved Toyota 4Runner hydroplaned, and I lost control, smashing into the center divider and spinning around three times, hitting the center divider yet again with every turn. My air bag had gone off, and I wasn't injured—but I was stuck in the fast lane of a major freeway during a complete downpour. I needed immediate assistance, so I did what any normal person would do. I called my mom.

MOM: Hello?

ME: Mom?

MOM: Yes?

ME: Hi, it's Danielle.

MOM: I only have one daughter, Danielle.

ME: Oh, right. Anyway, I was just in a really bad car accident on the freeway. I'm fine, though.

MOM: Oh, my God! Danielle, are you OK? Are the police on their way?

ME: I don't know.

MOM: Did you call them?

ME: No, I called you first.

MOM: Danielle Christine, hang up this phone right now and call nine-one-one! Why would you call me first?

I know it sounds silly, but I can't help it—when disaster strikes, my first instinct is always to call my mom. One time, a man was yelling and screaming at me while approaching my car with a steel baseball bat. I immediately called my mom, and not because she's Liam Neeson in *Taken* or anything. She's just my mom, and I'm (maybe) a little overly dependent.

Anyway, back to the freeway. I called the police, but in the meantime, I was stuck like a sitting duck in moving traffic. The visibility was incredibly low, and I was terrified that someone would rear-end me at high speed and I'd go soaring across all five lanes of the freeway. Only one person stopped to make sure I was OK: Jared Leto. (Yes, in LA, Academy Award winners just show up in times of need. Not really, but can you imagine?) I had never met Jared, but he noticed my destroyed car and pulled up next to me, gesturing for me to roll down my window.

JARED LETO: Hey. Pretty bad accident, huh? Are you OK?

ME: Yeah, it was pretty scary. Yes, I'm OK.

JARED: Do you want me to call the police for you?

ME: I already did, but thank you for asking.

JARED: OK, I hope your day gets better.

Then he rolled up his window and drove away. Jared Leto made me a forever fan that day. Who am I kidding? After falling in love with him as Jordan Catalano, I was already a forever fan, but it was still a very nice thing to do.

After my car had been towed, my mom had come to pick me up so I could make it to the *Boy Meets World* set for work, and Rider Strong drove me home from work. That night, over dinner with my family, we discussed what we were going to do since I was going to be without a car for a few weeks. I wasn't old enough to rent a car, so my dad generously offered to let me borrow his brand-new car, and he would drive a rental. The next day, my dad handed me his keys and told me to be careful. I made it to work without incident.

After work was a different story. I decided to stop at a local clothing store on my way home. The underground parking garage was steep and had a lot of turns. Thanks to my lack of skill and my desire to hug the right side of the road, I scraped the entire right side of his car across one of the curved garage walls. In an attempt to remove myself from the situation, I put the car in reverse—more scraping. I put the car in drive and inched forward—even more scraping. In a complete panic, I parked the car and jumped out, screaming for help. A man who was working in valet came over to help me. He was a much more experienced driver and somehow got my dad's car off the garage wall without any more damage. I thanked him profusely and drove back to my parents' house.

The whole way home, I contemplated how I was going to tell them. OK, honestly, I was trying to figure out a way I could avoid telling them, but there was none. I parked the car along the right side of the garage and hoped no one would notice before I could explain what happened. I came clean about the fiasco at dinner, and to their credit, neither my mom nor my dad murdered me. My dad put his head down with his fingers on the bridge of his nose, and my mom just looked at me and shook her head. The next day, my dad brought his car into the body shop, and my mom drove me to work. They removed me from their car insurance, and I was never allowed to drive one of their cars again. Gosh, they are such jerks, right? Just kidding. Don't ever let me borrow your car.

Unfortunately for my parents, I started making their lives difficult long before I learned to drive. When I was a little girl in the neon-hued mid-'80s, one of my favorite things to do was to help my mom get ready for an evening out. My parents didn't go out alone very often, choosing instead to spend time with my brother and me as a family, but when they did, I was her personal stylist. Usually, she would direct me to her closet and point out which fabulous dress—resplendent with shoulder pads, no doubt—she had decided to wear, and then I was responsible for selecting the appropriately matching panty hose (a *must* in the '80s), purse, jewelry, and shoes she should wear with it. This meant that if she was wearing a pink dress, I would find her pink panty hose (oh, yes, those actually existed), her pink purse, her gold jewelry, and her pink shoes. The '80s took its matching *seriously*. Playing the part of stylist was incredibly fun, because aside from feeling like I was really contributing to her look for the evening, I also got to play dress-up with all of my favorite clothes and accessories that my mom owned (like her pair of black snakeskin stilettos that dipped low around the toes and showcased excellent toe cleavage—I still dream about those shoes).

One day, my mom came home with a brand-new dress for a party she was attending with my dad. It was gorgeous, and I so badly wanted to try it on—which was ridiculous, because I was no more than four years old, and there wasn't a chance in the world that this dress was going to even remotely fit me. But the heart wants what the hearts wants, and I wanted to put that dress on my little body and dance around like a grown-up. My mom had always let me play in her closet, so I didn't see any reason this time would be any different—but it was.

My mom didn't shop for herself very often, and this particular dress was fresh from the store and still wore its price tag. She wasn't set to wear the dress for another couple of weeks and certainly didn't want her sticky-fingered child to play in it before she had even had a chance to wear it. Obviously, this all makes sense to me *now*, but at the time, none of it made sense. In my eyes, my mom had turned into a child-hating ogre and clearly wanted to torture me by bringing home a gorgeous dress that was off limits to me. I begged and begged to put the dress on, and she kept saying no. After a few fruitless minutes of begging, I exploded into a tantrum and demanded that she let me try on her dress through a stream of never-ending tears.

She lost her patience and yelled, "*No*, Danielle. How many times do I have to tell you *no?*"

*The first outfit I ever put together on my own. My mom
knew it was going to be good blackmail later in my life, so
she took a picture that could last forever.*

I was shocked. How could she do this to me? In my bro-
kenhearted-little-girl voice, I replied, "After everything I do for
you!" and ran off to my room. I don't know where I learned that
line, but I love that at four years old I was pretty sure that in
my relationship with my mom, *I* was the one doing everything
for *her.* I guess it's safe to say I've had a flair for the dramatic my
whole life.

As I got older, I became just as obsessed with putting my
own outfits together.

You can see that they weren't always "hits," but that has never stopped me from loving fashion. Now, when I tell you that I love fashion, I just mean that I greatly appreciate a well-put-together look. I do not mean to imply that I'm particularly good at it. I'm not. I'm terrible at putting together a complete ensemble that looks good on me, but that has never stopped me from doing it anyway (unfortunately).

Fashion lingo has never been a strong suit of mine, either. When I was ten, my mom actually had to tell me that "panty hose" was not plural for "panty hoe." She was teaching me how to delicately bunch a pair of panty hose down by my toes and slowly slide them up my leg to avoid snags.

"So, I take one panty hoe at a time," I started.

"Panty hose," she interrupted.

"Yeah, I know. But I'm doing them one leg at a time, so it's panty hoe," I quipped.

She burst into hysterical laughter, because she was instantly aware that her daughter was a moron.

Many years later, I got into a conversation in Bloomingdale's with a young woman working in the department that sold Elie Tahari. She was very passionate about fashion and clothes, and I was merely looking for a black cocktail dress. I didn't see anything I liked, but she kept insisting that I try on a few pieces. I declined politely and started to walk away—which she was not happy about.

"You know, Elie Tahari makes some of the highest-quality clothing in this store," she said.

Not really knowing how to respond to that comment, and certainly not wanting to offend a designer who was *nowhere near me,* I said, "Oh, I know. I love her stuff."

Her beady eyes were suddenly filled with hatred, and she informed me, "Elie Tahari is *a man.*"

Clearly having made a huge faux pas, I did what any normal person would do and ran out of the store, never to return again.

Long after I had outgrown my *Thriller* T-shirt, I got to work with some incredibly talented stylists on *Boy Meets World.* Certainly, not every outfit Topanga wore was a winner, but overall,

I mean, what is this look about? Nice mock turtleneck and white belt. At least Andrew Keegan looks good.

I loved her style. During the first season of the show, I wore as many dresses (*lace!*) with leggings and boots as I possibly could. That was my favorite season one look, and I replicated it in my personal life regularly. In the mid-'90s, Topanga's style evolved from bohemian chic to modern, and crop tops were all the rage at that time. In those years, I regularly wore high-waisted pants with colorful shirts tied up around my belly button.

Despite a few misses in the wardrobe department, Topanga's style has proven to be more evergreen than anything the boys got stuck with. Ben and Rider were constantly wearing layers upon layers of oversized shirts, some of them complete with dinosaurs.

Rider wearing at least two shirts and a vest.

By the time I turned seventeen, I had been working consistently for six years. I knew how much money I was making per episode, and I knew that it was *a lot*, especially for my age. But I never really understood how much money I had, because I didn't personally handle my own finances. That job fell to my responsible parents, who made investments for me and gave me an "allowance" from my own earnings. My allowance was more than what most children my age were given, but it was still rather menial. They figured that I didn't really need much money to spend willy-nilly, and they were right. We had lunch catered every day on set, and my parents paid for all the bills at home. My mom called my allowance "mad money," and I could spend it on whatever I wanted. Usually, that money went to movies, music, clothes, and Ice Blended coffees at Coffee Bean & Tea Leaf.

I started to think of my money as some unknown dollar amount that lived in a cloud in the sky. When I turned eighteen, I got my first credit card and had way too much time to spend shopping. I developed the irresponsible, bratty, and entitled habit of buying clothes and shoes that I didn't need, only to let them sit in my closet for months with the price tags on. Eventually, my closet would get full, and I'd have to clean it out and give all my new clothes away to friends and Goodwill so I could make room for *more* clothes. One year, I bought a pair of leather pants from a super-fancy store on Sunset Boulevard in a swanky area of Los Angeles. These pants cost well more than a thousand dollars, but I intended to wear them to the MTV Video Music Awards (VMAs), so I rationalized that it was an appropriate occasion to splurge on my outfit. I mean, I *was* going to be photographed in whatever I wore, so it shouldn't be something cheap and unattractive, I told myself. I did indeed wear those leather pants to the VMAs, and the minute I stepped out of the car, the zipper ripped wide open. I took a few strategically placed photos on the red carpet and then went inside the venue and watched the whole show with a broken zipper. Let's say that was the universe telling me never to spend that much money on a pair of pants—ever again.

Another bad habit I developed was not asking what something cost if the price wasn't readily available on the tag. I just assumed that the item couldn't be *too much*, right? Wrong.

When I turned twenty-two, I bought a condominium. My parents had been telling me for years that I should stop paying rent and buy a house, but it just seemed like such a big commitment. I mean, you can buy a pair of pants one day and decide you don't like them the next and just *get rid of them.* You can't do that with a home. But it was time to grow up and invest my money in something that had long-term value—unlike clothes.

Immediately after purchasing my condo, I went furniture shopping. My first order of business was to find a bed I loved. I am a *huge* fan of sleeping. If sleeping was an event in the Olympics, I would be the Michael Phelps of it. In my opinion, one of the key components of thoroughly enjoying the time you spend sleeping is having a bed that you can't wait to crawl into. After doing my due diligence and researching all the beds on the market, I ordered a humongous king-sized canopy bed. Naturally, when you're five-foot-one and single, you need the largest bed readily available. Unfortunately, there was a three-month wait for my gigantic bed, so I was forced to continue sleeping on my full-size mattress—placed, *sans* box spring, directly on the floor of my bedroom—for the foreseeable future.

In the meantime, my new bed was going to require a new mattress. A few months earlier, I had stayed at a W Hotel in New York and had never slept on such a divine mattress. The W Hotel, it turns out, actually sells the mattresses they use in their rooms. (I hope it's obvious that they sell new mattresses and not the ones other people have slept on, because that would just be yucko.) I ordered a king-size mattress and box spring, two king-size down pillows, and four standard pillows. Was that a lot of pillows? Perhaps, but like most sane people, I like comfort, and therefore, I like pillows. I was drooling at the thought of my bed arriving. I was gonna sleep in that bed so hard it wasn't going to know what hit it.

One afternoon while driving down Melrose Avenue—a very popular shopping area in LA—I saw a sign in the window of a home-decorating store that said, "Going Out of Business! 75% Off Storewide!" Considering that I had a new home that required some décor and only a fool would walk away from a seventy-five percent price cut, I thought I should check it out.

I walked into the store and immediately liked what I saw. They had beautiful artwork, fancy bathroom faucets, soft towels, and luxurious sheets. Buying luxurious sheets seemed like a no-brainer to me; I had a new bed on the way, and sheets I can't wait to dive into happen to be one of my life's greatest pleasures. I noticed that the sheets didn't come in a set like I had expected them to. Every piece was packaged separately: fitted sheet, flat sheet, and pillow cases. I thought this seemed odd, because I couldn't imagine a scenario where someone would walk into a store and decide to buy just one piece from what seemed like a set. Whatever. Whether or not I should buy the sheets was not even up for debate; in my mind, I already owned them.

I walked around the rest of the store to see if there was anything else I desired and noticed something a little strange. There weren't prices on anything. I looked at almost every item they had in the store, and not one thing was marked with a price. For a brief moment, this concerned me, but then I remembered the sign outside the store: seventy-five percent off storewide. Even if something had been ridiculously overpriced when they were in business, how overpriced could something be when it was seventy-five percent off?

It should be known that I was *completely* out of my element in this store. I had never owned a home, and therefore I didn't know the first thing about decorating one. I certainly didn't know what was considered a "reasonable price" for anything. When I lived at home, my parents always paid for any necessary household items, as parents usually do. Then, when I moved out of their house and into a rented apartment, I took my bed, mattress, towels, and sheets with me. One benefit of renting an apartment is that you don't need to bring a sink or a toilet with you; those items are waiting patiently for your arrival and ready to be used—again. (I do, however, highly recommend changing the toilet seat, because, gross.) For this newly purchased home, I had just paid twenty-seven hundred dollars for my king-size mattress and box spring, and I thought that was outrageous— unless you were a professional sleeper, like I fancied myself to be. Not to mention, you're supposed to keep a mattress for eight years (mine is ten years old now; am I a disgusting slob person?), so really, it was an investment in the future of my sleep, and I really could not compromise on something so valuable.

I decided that I was going to buy my insanely soft, gorgeous sheets and head home. I walked to the front of the store and put my sheets on the counter. The man who rang me up told me that he was crazy about the sheets I was buying and that I had exqui-site taste. I liked him already. I told him that I had just bought a new house and couldn't wait to put them on my bed. "Girl, these sheets are the absolute best in the world, and to be getting them at such a bargain is insane," he said. Now I was even more excited. I still didn't know what the final cost of my sheets was, but I was getting them for a *bargain*! My mom was going to be so proud of me for being frugal.

"OK, you got a flat sheet, a fitted sheet, two king pillow

cases, and four standard pillow cases," said the nice man behind the counter. "Your total is three thousand dollars even."

What happened next can only be described as an out-of-body experience. My brain was yelling something like *What the hell? Did he just say three thousand dollars? You clearly cannot pay this for a set of sheets!* but my body was moving as if nothing out of the ordinary had just happened. My hands grabbed my wallet and removed my credit card. I actually handed that credit card to the man who thought three-thousand-dollar sheets were a bargain and didn't utter a word. I signed my receipt and walked as quickly as possible to my car.

I sat in the front seat and started talking out loud to myself. "Maybe three thousand dollars is a normal price for super-luxurious sheets, Danielle. Just call your mother. She will have answers." I called my mom.

MOM: Hello?

ME: Mom, let's say you wanted to buy new sheets and you wanted really nice ones—like super-nice ones. The nicest sheets you've ever felt in your whole life. How much do you think those would cost?

MOM: I don't know, Danielle. Really nice sheets can be expensive. How much did you pay?

ME: Mom, these sheets I just bought were incredibly expensive. I didn't think anything could possibly be this expensive, and I supposedly got them for seventy-five percent off.

MOM: How much did you pay for the sheets, Danielle?

ME: How much would you guess I paid for really expensive sheets?

MOM: I don't know. What's the thread count?

ME: I have no idea! They're really nice. The nicest. You're gonna want to come sleep in my bed, that's how nice they are.

MOM: You bought sheets, and you don't even know what their thread count is?

ME: I don't even know what that means, Mom! Now, tell me, how much would you expect to pay for expensive sheets?

MOM: Oh, God. You're really going to make me tell you a price? I already know you paid too much.

ME: Hey, don't use your knowledge of my ridiculous shopping habits against me. Please, I need you to tell me what I should have paid for these sheets.

MOM: OK. If I were buying very expensive, really nice sheets, I would assume that they were somewhere around four or five hundred dollars.

I swear on everything I love that I almost passed out. I kept reliving the moment I stupidly handed my credit card over to the man behind the counter, wondering how I could have possibly been so insane as to pay three thousand dollars for a set of sheets.

I drove to my completely bare home and sat in a lawn chair that I had put in the family room. I looked around, and the realization that I did not have a couch, a coffee table, or a desk hit me. However, I was the new owner of a set of *three-thousand-dollar sheets for a bed I did not even have yet*! I immediately went into self-preservation mode. I started thinking about how I could get myself out of this situation and return the sheets. Even though the man who helped me at the store had already told me that there were no returns or exchanges (because they were going out of business and giving people *such great bargains* already?), I checked my receipt anyway. Sure enough, "No returns or exchanges" was printed just below my ridiculous total.

Sadly, I did return those sheets. I never had an opportunity to sleep on them and find out if they were so pricey because they turned one's hair into strands of gold, because I did what any normal, self-respecting person would do in my situation. I lied. I called the store in semifake tears (they were only semifake because I was partially crying about the fact that I was a hideous monster who thought three-thousand-dollar sheets could ever be considered acceptable) and told them this tale.

ME: Hi. I was in your store a little bit ago and bought some very nice sheets. Unfortunately, I just came home and found out that my husband was laid off today. I feel incredibly guilty for spending three thousand dollars on these sheets, and there is no way I can keep them now. I'm very sorry, but is there any way you can make an exception to the no-return policy?

By some miracle, they believed me. The man on the phone was very sympathetic, which made me feel terrible, because I knew I was a big stinky-faced liar. Even though that store should have caved in on itself for thinking anyone (other than me) would be stupid enough to believe that three-thousand-dollar sheets were normal, much less a bargain at seventy-five percent off, I still feel a little guilty that I lied to save myself from my own mistake. I said a *little* guilty, because, seriously, what were they thinking?

I am now a pretty frugal shopper. I don't hesitate to buy new things when I legitimately need them, but I no longer hand over my credit card without asking the cost of something. And you'll be pleased to know that I have found sheets that are equally luxurious at Bed Bath & Beyond for one hundred fifty dollars. Do you know what that comes out to? Ninety-five percent off! I win, store that's out of business, so you can shove it.

CHAPTER 5

WANNABE JOCK

Ever since I was a little girl, I've enjoyed sports. Primarily, I enjoy watching professional football and professional basketball. If you follow me on Twitter (@daniellefishel, what are you waiting for?), you know that I am a die-hard Dallas Cowboys and Los Angeles Lakers fan—which, for those of you who are sports-illiterate, are football and basketball teams, respectively.

I initially got into sports because my dad is very athletic and loves to spend his weekends parked in front of the television, watching anything and everything that is going on in the world of sports. My dad worked long hours during the week (and often on weekends), so I cherished quality time with him. Some of my earliest memories are of us watching Magic Johnson and the Lakers take on Larry Bird and the Boston Celtics. We also watched the Los Angeles Rams football games before they picked up and moved to St. Louis in 1994. When they moved, my dad was bitter. He felt like he could no longer root for them and instead started rooting for the Dallas Cowboys. I'm sure the fact that they had won Super Bowl championships in 1992 and 1993 had nothing to do with that decision. (Right, Dad?) Anyway, I jumped on the Big D bandwagon, too, and have never looked back, even though that bandwagon father of mine has since gone back to being a Rams fan, for some reason.

There's absolutely no father/daughter rivalry about this at all—can you tell?

Over the years, I've learned to play a few sports, too. I've been in gymnastics and have played soccer, softball, bowling (does that count as a sport?), ping-pong (does *that* count as a sport? I'm really reaching here, folks), golf, and, well, that's about it. Unfortunately, I can't say I'm great at any of them. I mean, I'm not terrible; I can throw a nice spiral with a football, I can play catch with a baseball, I can still do the splits (if I don't have anywhere I need to walk the next day), I have been known to kick butt at ping-pong, and my golf game is improving, albeit slowly. But not excelling at something doesn't mean I don't still enjoy playing. I'm competitive, and even if I don't end up winning, I love the opportunity to try.

Speaking of trying, check out the photos of Rider and Ben trying to beat me at arm wrestling.

When I was in elementary school, we always played Red Rover during recess. There are probably quite a few of you who don't know what Red Rover is, because it can be a bit aggressive,

and most schools don't allow it to be played anymore. Red Rover is a game where kids stand next to each other in two opposing lines about thirty feet apart. Then all of the kids in both lines hold hands to create a "chain link" of arms. One line is usually called the East line, and the other is called the West line. One at a time, one of the lines, let's say the East line for example, sings, "Red Rover, Red Rover, send Danielle right over." (They don't always sing the name Danielle, but this is my book, so I'm going to use my name. When you write a book, you can use your name if you'd like. You're welcome.) Then Danielle is supposed to run from the West line to the East line and try to break through two players' linked arms. If Danielle is successful in doing this (of course, I am—I mean, of course, *she* is), she gets to pick a player to go back to the West team with her. The whole goal is eventually to get every person onto your team to prove that you are strong and brave. Or something like that—I don't really know.

One day, during a particularly riveting game of Red Rover, one of my female friends went running over to break the chain of arms between two boys on the opposing team. They were much bigger and stronger than she was, and they clotheslined her. My poor little friend fell to the ground, gasping for air. (I don't remember her name, so we'll call her Danielle. Just kidding; we'll call her Stacy.) One of the boys, who doesn't deserve a mention here, started laughing in her face and calling her a "whiny baby." (I don't remember his name, either, to be honest; we'll just call him Dan. Ha! See what I did there?) I was so furious at him that I ran from my team over to his team and told him he needed to apologize to her or I was going to tell on him. Unlike Dan, I was a good kid and did not like to get in trouble with anyone, so that threat would have scared me straight. It didn't scare him, though. Nope, Dan socked me right in the eye as hard as he could. I immediately started crying, took Stacy's hand, and left the game with her. I thought about going to tell someone what had happened, but I really didn't want to deal with the wrath of Dan for the rest of my elementary school days. Any boy who thinks nothing of socking a girl in the face is obviously a sociopath, right?

Later, when my mom picked me up from school, I had a full shiner. My whole eye was puffy and black and blue. My mom demanded to know what happened, and because I believed her to be a rational woman who had a heart, I told her the story. I also told her that under no circumstances was she "allowed" to tell anyone about it. We were all going to forget that this had happened, and I was going to avoid Dan like the plague for the rest of my life. Problem solved. But that's not what happened. I wrongfully assumed my mom would handle this situation like I did—like a big wuss. No, no, no. Not my mother. She took me home and put a bag of frozen peas on my eye and told me to be ready to leave the house in thirty minutes.

"Where are we going?" I asked.

"We're going to CCD, and I am going to have a word with Dan's father," she said.

"Mom, no!" I yelled.

Until I was about ten years old, my family attended a Catholic church, which meant I was required to attend catechism class, or CCD, on Wednesdays after school. I really disliked having to go to CCD after my regular school day, and my mom didn't particularly like having to take me, so like the horrible Catholics we were, she wouldn't always make me go. On the day of the Red Rover Incident, I hadn't been to CCD in a few weeks. I barely remembered that good ol' "Dan the Girl Puncher" was in my class—but my mom remembered *everything*, apparently.

I begged and pleaded to no avail, and my mom drove me to CCD and dragged me out of our car and toward the church classroom. Dan wasn't there yet, so I prayed extra hard that Dan's parents had decided they wanted to skip CCD so they could spend a lovely afternoon with their psychopath child and I could be spared this horrendous embarrassment.

God did not answer my prayer that day.

My mom was still fuming. She stood outside the CCD classroom with her arms tightly folded, every now and then muttering something like "Who does he think he is?" or "I should punch *him* in the face." Even though I was furious that she was putting me through this awkward encounter, there was a part of me that loved seeing my mom this worked up. I knew that my parents loved me, but every now and then—usually when something either really amazing or really awful happened—I got to peer into the deep, dark depths of their love. And until I have kids of my own, I don't think I'll ever even scratch the surface of how profound that love is.

Dan and his dad started across the parking lot and headed right toward us. My mom dropped her arms and took my hand. *Please let this be swift and painless*, I thought to myself while staring at the ground as we walked. When we got to within ten feet of them, I looked up and made eye contact with Dan. His eyes were squinting, and he was scowling with disdain. This couldn't end well for me.

"Sir, look at my daughter's face," my mom said in her sternest voice. "Do you see that black eye? Take a good hard look at it, and then you tell me if you think it is acceptable to raise a son who punches little girls in the eye."

Dan's dad looked shocked. "Dan, did you punch Danielle in the *face*?" he asked. I wasn't thrilled with the way he said "face." It was as if Dan and his dad had a previous discussion about where it was acceptable to punch a girl and where it wasn't—and face was apparently one of the no-no's.

Dan, to his credit, didn't try to lie. He hung his head in—what I perceived to be—shame and nodded his head. Dan's dad took Dan by the hand and told him that this was completely unacceptable behavior and he was going to be severely punished. I hoped this meant he was going to be severely punished *right now, in front of Danielle*, but it did not. Dan's dad apologized to my mom and me, and then he made Dan apologize to both of us. My mom accepted and said that she hoped Dan really would be punished, because it sure would be a shame if this event had to be reported to our school principal and Dan was expelled from elementary school. And then Dan's dad and my mom just sent Dan and me on our merry way into CCD, where Dan gave me the evil eye for a straight hour. I don't know what Dan's parents did to punish him but, other than the occasional stink-eye from across the playground, he actually left me alone, and I never exchanged words (or fists) with him again.

For a few years, I was conflict-free on the playground. Then, one day while playing softball in middle school PE, I went up to bat and hit a grounder out to right field. I started running around the bases and was around first when the second baseman caught the ball from the right outfielder, and I knew he needed to tag me with the ball before I touched base if he wanted to get me out. The normal thing to do would have been to slide into second base before he could tag me out with the ball. But this was middle school, and I had other classes to go to before the day was over, and I didn't want to be a dirty mess for the rest of the day; I mean, I wasn't winning the World Series here. So I just kept running for second base—and the baseman who was holding the softball. When I got right in front of him, he jetted his arm out and smashed my chest with the ball, *hard*. Really hard. So hard that I couldn't breathe; the wind was knocked out of me. I bent over and tried to catch my breath while he laughed and said it was an accident. My teacher came over to check on me, but at this point, everyone on the field was laughing, and I was embarrassed. I stood upright and walked over to the second baseman and kicked him in his "private area" as hard as I could.

Now, I'm not a boy, clearly, but I hear that it hurts extremely badly when this part of the male body gets abused. I understand that, completely. But try explaining that to my developing chest!

The second baseman doubled over in excruciating pain. I instantly felt terrible. It was very apparent in that moment that my pain was at most one-third of what he seemed to be experiencing; he was coughing and had rolled onto the ground in the fetal position. Our (male) PE teacher looked at me like I was possibly the spawn of Satan. I hugged myself to casually remind him why I had kicked in the first place. Our PE teacher wasn't just angry with me, and he yelled at both of us. He decided not to send either one of us to the principal's office, and my fellow student and I exchanged apologies. Although my pain level was decreasing rapidly, it did appear that the second baseman was not as lucky. Every time I saw him for the rest of the day, he was hunched over like he had a terrible stomach ache. I swore I would never kick another male in the privates ever again, unless, of course, I was being attacked. In that case, a swift kick seemed debilitating enough for a woman to get away from her attacker, and I thought of it as a good learning experience—albeit a painful one for my male classmate.

You'd think my previous elementary school experience with Dan would have permanently scared me away from the idea of giving or receiving punches, but it did not. Years later, when I was in high school, I became obsessed with working out. My parents had a gym in our home, and I would work out any time I had the chance. My dad was an avid exerciser, and sometimes he and I would work out together. It was fun. We were both competitive, and I loved to see how much weight he could bench-press, leg-press, and squat. Of course, I was never able to come anywhere near doing the same weight he did, but I still liked to compare. I tried to compete with my dad over everything: how fast we could run, how much weight we could lift, whether I could beat him in arm wrestling. My mom was not thrilled with my competitive nature and wondered how it was possible that she, the ultimate girly-girl, had given birth to a daughter who suddenly desired to be as manlike as her father. It was during this time that my mom told me that boys didn't usually like it when a girl could beat them in weight lifting and arm wrestling. I still didn't care—and I loved boys, so that says a lot about my desire to beat them in everything.

One Saturday afternoon, my dad and I were working out together in the gym. He was walking on the treadmill, and I was doing leg lifts and reverse curls on the leg extension machine. When he finished walking, he put on some boxing gloves and started shadow boxing. Excited to have yet another thing to compete over, I stopped my leg exercises and asked him if we could trade a few punches. I put the boxing gloves on my hands and delivered a few punches to his arms, and he was impressed with how strong I was. He told me to hit him as hard as I could in the arm a couple of times. Then I got tired.

"OK, your turn, Dad. Hit me as hard as you can," I said.

"Danielle, I'm not going to hit you." He laughed.

This did not make me very happy. "What, because I'm a girl, you don't think I can take a punch to the arm?" I quipped.

He told me that being a girl had nothing to do with it and that he just didn't want to hurt me. I assured him that he was not going to hurt me and that I could take a punch.

Eventually, he relented and took a few light jabs at my right arm, but that wasn't going to work for me.

"Dad, stop hitting me like a baby. Hit me as hard as you can—I promise I won't get hurt." I'm not sure why that worked, but it did. I bet all parents have a desire to punch their kids as hard as they can at least once. How could they not? I imagine kids bring a whole lot of joy most of the time but can also completely suck the life and sanity out of a normal person occasionally.

My dad said, "All right. One punch, OK?" I nodded and braced myself for what came next, a swift punch to my flexed right arm. Instantly, I felt teeth-chattering, brain-shaking pain and numbness—all over. I swear my head must have looked like a bobble head, and I had no control over it. I just stood there, shaking and frozen. My dad ripped his gloves off, grabbed my shoulders, looked me in the eye, and asked if I was OK. I started smiling while my teeth were still chattering, and I tried to bring feeling back into my arm.

"I didn't really think you'd hit me as hard as you could, but I'm glad you did. I definitely won't ever ask you to do that again, though," I chattered.

"I'm glad to hear that. And Danielle, that wasn't even close to as hard as I can punch. Make sure you tell your future boyfriends," he said as he gave me a hug.

While I don't condone violence, there's something nice about knowing that if anyone messes with me, my dad could easily beat the crap out of them—and then go to jail, because you're not allowed to beat the crap out of people. Yay! Family stories!

As freaked out as my dad was by the punching incident, he didn't exactly learn his lesson. About a year later, he took me out to play tennis. We had a community tennis court at the end of our street, and he would regularly take his ball machine out to practice returns. My dad was exceptionally good at tennis and even won a few singles and doubles tournaments at our local club. I was not that good at it and could never master a one-handed forehand. I always played with both hands on my racket for my forehand and backhand shots. This made me fairly slow to return balls, and I knew I wasn't much of a match for my dad. In typical me fashion, I didn't like this very much. Instead of just rallying back and forth, I asked my dad to serve me a few balls as fast as he could; he had a very fast serve that I rarely got to see because he always took it easy on me. He told me to get ready to return his serve, so I set myself up in the corner opposite his and got my two-handed forehand shot ready. I watched him throw the ball into the air and hit it with his racket.

That's the last thing I saw. The next thing I knew, his tennis ball was perfectly wedged in my right eye socket. My eyeball had never felt so much pain, and I clamped my hand over it and screamed. Panicked, my dad came running over to make sure he hadn't blinded me. I peeled my hand off my eye so he could look at it. I was fine: no popped blood vessels, no instant bruising, just some blurry vision and white stars when I closed my eyes.

Suddenly, I started laughing. "Dad, how did that ball get to my eye so quickly? I didn't even see it cross the court."

He cracked up. "Danielle, you just stood there—like, you didn't even move a muscle. I don't think tennis is your sport. Let's go home."

Sadly, when it comes to sports, spectating seems to be as dangerous as participating for me. When I was in my mid-twenties, I started going to golf tournaments with my boyfriend at the time. We both enjoyed watching Tiger Woods compete, and he has an annual tournament called the World Challenge at the Sherwood Country Club, which is not too far from where I was living. My boyfriend and I decided it would be a fun weekend activity to go to the tournament and follow Tiger from hole to hole. While it is absolutely impressive to watch the pros drive, chip, and putt like I could only dream of doing, it is also a really long day out in the heat, and I had stupidly worn jeans because it was cold in the morning when I got dressed.

Around noon, after drinking three bottles of water and walking consistently for four hours, I needed to use the bathroom. I asked someone where I could find the nearest restroom, and he told me there was a port-a-potty a few holes away. I wasn't that excited about having to walk ahead a few holes to use a port-a-potty, only to have to turn around and walk all the way back to keep following Tiger. I decided I didn't really need to go to the bathroom that badly and that I could wait until we got closer to port-a-potty headquarters.

About an hour later, and only one hole closer, I could no longer wait. I had to pee so badly that I could hardly stand upright. I told my boyfriend and his dad, who had joined us for the day, that I was going to have to run for my life to the port-a-potties and that I'd be back. I walked as fast as my little legs could walk. I tried jogging a bit, but that was too painful. My mantra became, *Danielle, you will not pee your pants. Don't you even dare.*

Finally, I made it to the bathrooms. Apparently, I was not the only one who needed to relieve herself, because there were easily fifteen people in line in front of me. I started doing a little pee-pee dance in hopes it would prevent me from wetting my pants. Miraculously, it worked. I made it into a port-a-potty and was happy to see that it was pretty nice, as port-a-potties go. The moment I closed the door, I flipped the lock and unbuttoned my jeans. I got into the hovercraft position—just like in my ill-fated audition, except this time I was actually peeing. The first thing I noticed was not relief; it was the sound my urine was making as it hit the toilet bowl. It was louder than I thought it should have been, but I was just so happy to have not peed my pants I didn't care.

When I was done, I pulled up my jeans and realized they were sopping wet. I groaned loudly and turned around. There was a freaking toilet-seat *cover* in this fancy golf tournament port-a-potty, and apparently, the unnecessarily polite user before me had put the cover down. In my haste, I had not noticed this and had just peed directly onto the seat cover—which, in turn, funneled all of my urine directly into my jeans.

I tried to think of a way to get myself out of this horrendous situation, but there was none. I didn't have an extra pair of pants with me, I didn't have a sweater to tie around my waist, and walking around in my underwear didn't seem appropriate. So I did the only thing I could do: I washed my hands and exited the port-a-potty with the confidence of a Victoria's Secret model. Being careful not to make eye contact with anyone, I calmly and quickly walked over to my boyfriend and his father and told them what happened. We made the unanimous decision that we had to leave (ya think?). I sat down on a bench in my uncomfortably wet, pee-soaked jeans while my boyfriend went to the pro shop to buy a long-sleeved golf shirt. When he came back, I tied it around my waist, and we made the long walk back to the car. I rode home in a pair of basketball shorts my boyfriend had in his trunk. It was not my best look.

Because I am a glutton for punishment, I decided to take up *playing* golf a couple of years after that pee-soaked spectating incident. As a birthday gift to my dad, I booked us a round at our favorite local golf course and invited my usual golf partners, Tim and his dad, Mike. I didn't play particularly well all day, but it was nice to be outside, enjoying the company of three of my favorite men. When we got to the eighteenth hole, there was a huge flock of ducks sitting on the fairway that leads to the green. I looked at my dad and said, "Oh, God. What if I hit one of them with my ball?" My dad assured me that as long as I got loft on the ball, I wouldn't be killing any ducks that day. I wasn't convinced, though. I decided I would feel a lot better if I could simply get the ducks to waddle into the pond that was right behind them. I squawked and jumped and yelled at the ducks to move, but they refused to listen—they probably thought I was a maniac (everyone else on the golf course certainly did). In a last-ditch effort, I slowly drove my golf cart toward them, and that worked—the gaggle of ducks made their way into the pond. Proudly, I drove back to my ball, ready to take my shot.

DAD: You feel better now?

ME: Yes, much better. I knew I wouldn't hit a good shot if I was worried I'd hit one of them.

DAD: OK, then I won't screw you up by telling you that

all of the ducks went right back to the fairway after you drove away.

I turned around, and sure enough, all of those little ducks had hopped out of their pond and nestled comfortably back on the fairway. I mumbled a few obscenities and geared up to take my shot. *Just get loft under the ball, Danielle. Just get loft,* was all I could think to myself. I swung my club back and connected with the ball—poorly. I did get loft under my ball, but I didn't hit it hard enough. The ball hit the ground a few yards in front of the ducks before taking off like a bat out of hell—right into one duck's face. The ducks I managed to miss flew off, while the one injured duck tumbled onto its side, shaking its poor little head viciously. It's hard for me to remember what happened next because I was in absolute hysterics. Crying and screaming, I ran as fast as I could to the clubhouse to . . . Get help? Turn myself into the authorities? I have no idea why I thought someone at the clubhouse would be able to help that sad, wounded duck, but I did. When I made it to the front desk, I tried to explain what had happened, but they all just looked at me like I was speaking gibberish. To their credit, I probably was.

Ten seconds into my "I might be a duck murderer" rant, my dad walked in.

DAD: Danielle. Look out the window—right now.

ME: No, no, no. I don't want to see.

DAD: He's fine, Danielle. Look! He's getting up—*slowly*—but he's getting up.

I looked out the window, and bless his little duck heart, he was walking. He was slightly off balance but managed to make his way to the pond with his friends and swim around. I kept my eyes locked on him while my dad went to get my golf clubs from the fairway of the eighteenth green and throughout our outdoor lunch at the nearby restaurant. But eventually, all of the ducks started to look the same. I still felt awful, and whenever I think about that day, I shudder, but I am so relieved I hadn't killed or seriously injured him.

The next time I went to that golf course, the ducks had miraculously disappeared, and I've never seen them since. Either the golf course relocated the ducks to protect them from me, or the ducks decided all on their own that they didn't want to live in a place where that psychopath Danielle Fishel plays. I'd be willing to bet it's the latter.

I still haven't really found "my sport." Despite my less-than-stellar experiences, I still love to play golf and try to play about once a week—but I'm not really getting much better at it. I need to take lessons. In the meantime, I am perfectly happy watching the pros do their thing on television. It's fun to watch and is so much safer for those who are accident-prone like I am. I have never once been physically injured while watching TV.

I am way more proud of that than any sane person should be.

CHAPTER 6

NEVER TOO OLD

I was eighteen when *Boy Meets World* started its seventh season. I had graduated from high school, and I technically should have been starting college. But I had been going to school and working on *BMW* for six years, and the idea of starting college during our final season sounded . . . kind of unbearable. I know I told you that I loved high school, but it wasn't because of the academics. I loved school for the normal reasons: boys, friends, and the availability of cafeteria pizza. Any place that has pizza is a worthwhile place to be, in my opinion.

For years, my decision not to attend college ate at me. Didn't I want to develop a well-rounded education that I could carry with me for life? Didn't I want to have a solid game plan if I ever decided that I didn't want to be an actress anymore? Didn't I want to meet college boys and make college friends and eat college pizza? Of course I did. And that's when I knew I had to go back to school.

At twenty-three, I took my placement exams at a community college in Los Angeles called Santa Monica College (SMC). It was nerve-racking for me, because not only had I not been on a school campus since high school, but I was afraid that my identity as Topanga would follow me everywhere I went. I *loved* being known as Topanga, but I wanted people to want to get to know Danielle, too. I was hopeful that college would be that opportunity but nervous that other people wouldn't be accepting of me.

On the day of my math and English placement exams at SMC, I nervously walked alone across the campus. A group of guys noticed me and yelled, "Topangaaaaaa!" from across the quad, and everyone in the vicinity stopped what they were doing and looked at me. My face flushed, I smiled meekly, and I instantly put my head down as I increased my walking speed. Blending in was already not going as planned.

A few weeks later, I got the results of my placement exams and was given a date to enroll for the fall semester. I should have been excited to register, but I didn't do it. A thousand thoughts raced through my head: What if people made fun of me? What if people talked about me behind my back? What if I never made any friends and was completely isolated from everyone on campus? What if I didn't remember how to be a student? With the books, the notes, the studying, and the time-management skills, being a student is a lifestyle. I wasn't very good at it back in high school, so why on earth did I think I'd be better at it in college? And what if I hated it and wanted to drop out? At that time, I figured trying and not succeeding was much worse than simply never trying. So I made a million excuses and let four more years go by without enrolling in school.

During those four years, barely a day went by that I didn't regret not enrolling at SMC. When I turned twenty-seven, I realized I would have been *graduating* if I had enrolled and attended school full-time after taking my placement exams. It's not like I didn't have the time. I didn't even have a regular acting job, so I was basically consistently unemployed and uneducated, which sucked.

I felt about as low as I had ever felt. I felt like a loser. No job, no skills other than acting, no possibilities for work in the near future, and no college education. I thought about all of the times in my life that I had made the decision not to do something I really wanted to do. There was one common denominator in every instance: fear.

I was afraid of what people would think about me, afraid that people wouldn't like me, afraid that I wouldn't get good grades, afraid that I'd never get the chance to act again and would be unemployable for any other job for the rest of my life. I was terrified that I'd end up being regarded as a total failure by myself and my family. I was afraid of letting strangers down, letting my family down, and letting myself down.

But what exactly was that fear doing to help me? Absolutely nothing. I had simply avoided trying to better myself, and instead, I had jumped right to the failing. I realized that I didn't have anything to lose; everything I feared had already happened, because I wasn't even *trying* to change my situation. I was paralyzed by my own insecurities, and I was determined to quit being my own worst enemy.

I called my parents. I told them that I was done being afraid of everything that challenged me and that I had made the decision to go back to school. I asked my parents to stay on me about this decision, and if it seemed to them like I was getting ready to back out, please remind me that I was a big fat chicken and that I should go anyway.

I had enrolled in a community college, Santiago Canyon College (SCC), that was near my new house in Orange County, and my parents never needed to remind me that I was a big fat chicken. I signed up for only eight units, because I didn't want to be overwhelmed in my first semester of college. I knew from past experiences that feeling overwhelmed would only give me yet another excuse to back out. I was slowly learning how to set myself up for academic success.

Then the first day of school arrived in what seemed like a flash—and I missed it. I'm not sure why I wasn't more prepared (scared and in denial that I actually had to show up, maybe?), but I could have sworn I signed up for classes that were on Tuesdays and Thursdays. Stupidly, I waited until Monday at eleven

A.M. to get my backpack organized. The first thing I did was print my schedule so I could put it inside my notebook. That's when I noticed that I had a class at ten A.M. on Monday morning . . . and I was in bed. In my pajamas. At eleven A.M. Organizing my stupid backpack. The first day of class was almost over, and I had never shown up.

I panicked. I didn't know what to do. Should I take this as a sign and just never go? No. Yes. Maybe. *You big fat chicken.* No! I went to the school website, looked up my Monday teacher's email address, and emailed her. Her name was Dr. Anne Hauscarriague. Hauscarriague? Great. Now not only was I the slacker student who didn't show up for the first day of her class, but I was never going to be able to pronounce her name.

In my email, I apologized profusely and told her the truth about what happened. I also told her that I was twenty-seven and this was my first semester back at school since high school. I also told her that I was normally very conscientious and responsible and that my not showing up on the first day was not an accurate representation of who I am. I basically begged for another chance. First day of school, and I was already groveling. Maybe I should have continued to be a student at the University of Life, since I already seemed to stink at real college.

Dr. Hauscarriague wrote me back and said that students who miss the first day of school are usually dropped immediately. However, she still had seats available in her class and might be willing to give me another chance if I came to her office that day to go over what I missed earlier that morning. I agreed and went to school to meet her in her office.

During our face-to-face meeting, I apologized profusely again for missing her class. I found myself being very honest with her about my fears and concerns about starting such an important endeavor at twenty-seven years old. She told me that I had nothing to worry about and that people much older than I had gone back to school and been very successful. Apparently, I just needed to actually show up for class and do the work. Amazing!

Dr. H, as she became known, was incredible. She was approachable, helpful, funny, straightforward, and encouraging. She was never afraid to make a fool of herself if she thought it would help her students remember an important equation, and when students did particularly well on a test, she gave them pencils that had "Math rocks!" printed on the side. There have been quite a few teachers who have helped shape my life, and Dr. H was one of them.

After spending two surprisingly fun years at SCC, I graduated with my associate of arts degree and transferred to California State University, Fullerton (CSUF). On May 5, 2011, I turned thirty and was finishing up my first semester at CSUF. Just like she does every year, my mom took me out for birthday pancakes.

I'm not sure how our pancake tradition got started. We both love pancakes, but we try not to eat them on a regular basis for two reasons; one, they aren't exactly healthy, and two, we both feel the same way after we eat them. We're full all day until dinner, at which point we get the shakes, because we have very little nutrition in our systems but a whole lot of sugar. I douse my pancakes in syrup, and if you don't do the same thing, then I'm not sure why you're eating them. To me, a pancake is basically the vessel that carries gallons of syrup down my gullet, and that's the way I like it.

My mom is equally obsessed with "syrup vessels," and we can eat a lot of them, especially considering that we are not very big people. With my five-foot-one-*and-a-quarter*-inch height, I tower over her petite five-foot-tall frame. She weighs barely more than one hundred pounds, and I regularly hover somewhere between one hundred ten and one hundred fifteen pounds, depending on whether I am eating to live or living to eat at that particular time. I frequently bounce back and forth between the two. The point is, every time we order pancakes—*every single time*—the server asks us the same question: "Are you sure you want a *full stack* of pancakes? We offer a half stack." Who eats a half stack of pancakes? Children? Do we look like children? Of course we each want a full stack of pancakes, but when you make us spell it out like that, I feel like you're judging me. *Stop judging my pancake eating!* (I say this in my head, choosing to smile politely and say, "Yes, a full stack is fine, thank you," because that's called maturity. I think.)

On this particular birthday (just like every other birthday), I devoured my *full stack* of pancakes covered in syrup, said good-bye and thank you to my mom, and left for school. I had a big oral presentation to give that morning and wanted to have time to prepare before I went into class.

Well, I had intended to prepare, but when I got to school an hour early, I was hit by the pancake wall. My stomach was so full, and I was already coming down from my syrup sugar high. I parked my car in the school lot and went over my presentation out loud a couple of times. My car was so quiet, the air-conditioning felt so good, and, oh, hey, look, my seat even reclined! Yes, a nap was exactly what I needed. I set the alarm on my phone, rolled over onto my stomach, which is the only way I can sleep, and closed my eyes.

When my alarm went off, I was shocked to discover that I had apparently been hitting snooze for some time. I had five minutes to get my stuff together and get to class. I grabbed my notebook and my purse and locked my car. I got to class with one minute to spare.

I was the third person to present that day. When it was my turn, I stood up and walked to the front of the class. I noticed that some people were looking at me with semiconfused expressions. Two girls in the back of the room looked at me, then looked at each other and started laughing. My first thought was, *Do I have something stuck in my teeth?* But then I remembered that I had only eaten pancakes, which don't get stuck in teeth. I was fine.

My presentation went smoothly. I had nailed it and was pretty sure I could count on getting an A for that assignment.

Nothing made me happier than getting As. After years of primarily attending school for the social functions and activities, I was suddenly obsessed with being an outstanding student. It was annoying to everyone around me, excluding my teachers, and I was frequently annoyed with myself. I didn't know where this nerdy and Topanga-esque personality trait came from, but I think it had a lot to do with the fact that I really, really wanted to be there. It took determination, courage, and overcoming years of fear for me to be on that campus, and I wanted to make the most of it. I'm also competitive and looked at getting good grades as winning in the imaginary game of college. That's what you do when you get older. Make up imaginary games so you can win them.

When class was over, I walked to my car with a big smile on my face. I drove home and walked my dogs, Anna and Spike.

My neighbor came outside and made small talk for a few minutes. Then she asked, "Are you OK?"

I wanted to tell her that I was more than OK because I had just nailed a presentation at school, but I didn't. I said, "Yeah, of course. Why?"

She didn't really give me a solid answer but instead mumbled something about me looking like I had been crying. *Hmmm*, I thought. *That's weird.*

I took my dogs inside and went upstairs to put on my pajamas. It was only two o'clock in the afternoon, but that didn't stop me. Side note: When I'm home, it is guaranteed that I will be in my pajamas. I love pajamas. If I wake up and don't have to leave the house, I stay in my pajamas. If I do have to go somewhere in the morning, I put on regular clothes and then immediately come home and put my pajamas back on. I don't care if I'm only going to be home for an hour or two before I have to leave again—if I am home, I am in my pajamas. This book was written entirely in my pajamas.

Anyway, on my way to the closet, where I had left my pajamas, I caught a glimpse of myself in the mirror. I did look like I had been crying. I walked right up to my bathroom mirror and looked at my face. What was looking back at me wasn't pretty. I had mascara smeared halfway down my right cheek. My left eye was surrounded by mascara flakes, which made it look like I had a black eye. The blue dress I was wearing had a stain that stretched into a straight line down the front of my dress. It was syrup—which had ended up there because I had syrup in my freaking hair.

I had just been standing in front of my professor and forty other college students for ten minutes with syrup in my hair and down the front of my dress and mascara smeared all over my face. I wondered how this could have possibly happened, and it was in that instant that I realized I had not looked in the mirror, not even once, since I had left my house for pancakes earlier that morning. Excellent. On that day, my birthday, I had a rare day without vanity, and look where it got me. I told myself that I was never to be trusted around food again unless a mirror was nearby. Oh, and naps in the car were officially outlawed. I never did nap in my car before class again.

A year and a half later, I was enjoying the summer before my last semester of college. I'm not exactly sure how it started, but I had become completely infatuated with bowling. You've probably noticed by now that I have a bit of an obsessive personality. I can become obsessed with nearly anything—a TV show, a certain food, a particular sport, a beverage, a band or artist, books, and so on. I have been preoccupied with everything I just mentioned, and many others I did not mention, at one time or another. My obsessions come in waves, with very little warning about when they begin and when they might end. This particular summer, bowling was on my brain all the time.

One Friday evening, Tim and I went bowling with his family. There were six of us in our group, and we were all playing. We may have also consumed some adult beverages. I remember many Corona bottles covering our little table like a beer graveyard, interspersed with a few rocks glasses containing the remnants of my then-current beverage fixation, sugar-free Red Bull and vodka.

At some point, maybe one, or three, drinks later, I noticed that there was a family bowling in the lane next to us. They had a super-cute little boy who couldn't have been any more adorable trying to roll his heavy bowling ball down the long hardwood lane. I normally like kids, but when I've consumed an adult beverage, or three, I *really* like kids.

"Hi!" I said to the little kid next to me. I may have said it a little loudly. I'm actually one hundred percent sure I said it very loudly. All of a sudden, it occurred to me that I may have cursed when my bowling ball did not knock down all the pins during my turn, like I had planned it would in my head. I *despise* people who curse in front of little kids who are old enough to know what's being said. Now I was one of them. This issue must be rectified. I needed to prove to this small stranger that I was not some loser who didn't know how to use her words for good instead of evil. I was going to be his friend.

My adorable new friend's mother came over to her son and said, "Joshua, say hi," and he did. Within a few minutes, Joshua and I were laughing and having a grand old time.

"I can do the splits!" he said.

Of course, I told him that I did not believe this was true and that he was going to need to prove it to me.

Joshua plopped down into the splits, and I was amazed.

"Wow! That is so good. Wanna know something?" I said. He nodded his head. "I can do the splits, too."

What I should have said was *About twenty-five years ago, I was in gymnastics, and I learned how to do the splits.* I had an idea that I could still do them, because a few years earlier, yoga was my exercise obsession of choice. I was flexible a few years ago, so why wouldn't I be flexible now, right?

With the help of one, or three, Red Bull vodkas in my system, I plopped into split position. Joshua was impressed. He plopped into split position, too. This recurring plopping continued until we had dropped into the splits at least four different times. Joshua thought it was hilarious. So did Tim and his family, but they were laughing at me, not with me, like dear, sweet Joshua was.

Eventually, our game was over and it was time to take a cab home. I said good-bye to Joshua, and we left.

The next day, I was so sore I could barely move. "Tim, why do my legs feel like noodles?" I asked.

"Uh, because you dropped into the splits about a thousand times with a little kid last night," he said, snorting. Tim is prone to exaggeration, clearly.

"Oh, yeah. Of course, I remember. That was fun. Can you help me walk down the stairs?" I pleaded.

A month and a half later, summer was over and school was back in session. I had been asked by one of my favorite professors, Dr. Zettel-Watson (Dr. ZW), to be part of a small group of students working on the beginning stages of a very important grant proposal. There were two other students in this group: Dmitry, who had just graduated with his master's degree in psychology from CSUF, and Jarred, another psychology undergrad, just like me. We had three professors to report to: Dr. ZW, Dr. Wilson, and Dr. Horn-Mallers.

A few weeks into the semester, Dmitry, Jarred, and I had some good information that we were ready to present to our professors. We had a meeting in a conference room on campus scheduled for ten fifteen A.M. The three of us got there right at ten o'clock and waited for our professors to arrive.

Dr. ZW got there first. Shortly after, Dr. Horn-Mallers walked in. Dr. ZW introduced us to Dr. Horn-Mallers, and when I shook her hand, she looked at me and said, "I know you." I certainly didn't know her. I had never met her before. She asked if I had taken a class with her previously, and I told her I hadn't. She asked if I was sure, and I told her I was. This was getting uncomfortable. I needed to make a good impression on this woman. She was one of the leaders of this project that I had been selected for because of my good grades, work ethic, and drive. I was about to present some important research to her with my group, and I wanted her to like me.

Dr. Horn-Mallers was absolutely sure that she knew me. I sensed that she wasn't going to drop the topic unless she figured out how she knew me, so as awkward as it was to say, I said, "Well, I'm an actor, so maybe that's how you know me?"

"No, no, that's definitely not it," she said.

And then it happened. "Oh, I know where I know you from! You're the girl who did the splits with my son at the bowling alley a couple of months ago."

Noooooooooooo!

That is all I had running through my head. *Please let that not be true. Please don't tell me that a couple months ago, when I was loud and drinking at a bowling alley, I started doing the splits with my professor's son!*

I felt my face turn red. "Oh, right. That's right," I sputtered.

Sweetly, she said, "He didn't stop talking about you for days. You really made an impression."

Good Lord. I really made an impression. "Well," I began nervously. "That was fun, but I assure you, I have a more academic side, too." I don't think I was very convincing, but she took my word for it anyway.

The rest of the meeting went well. I was able to show that I was more than just a drunken bowler-slash-gymnast and that I would actually be a worthwhile contributor to the project. The rest of the semester went off without a hitch. I also, wisely, changed bowling alleys.

I graduated from college in fall 2012, when I was thirty-one years old. Making the decision to go to school was hard for me, but I wouldn't change a thing. I was constantly learning new things, meeting new people, working on exciting projects. Sure, it was a little scary, and it was more work than I could have ever prepared for, but I learned so much about myself. I learned that I have very good time-management skills and can succeed in a class even when I dislike the subject material. I know you're not reading this book because you're looking to be talked into something, but I have to say this: Going to school was the *best* thing I have ever done for myself. It was a present I didn't know I wanted and didn't know I'd ever receive. I challenged myself every day, and when I graduated, I could barely believe I had accomplished something so significant. I love my job, but absolutely no acting success will ever compare to the sense of accomplishment I have for graduating from college. I hope that if you have ever thought about going to college and talked yourself out of it for any reason, you believe me when I tell you that you can do it. You can, and you'll be thankful you did. I know I am.

CHAPTER 7

BEFORE THE RING

One of my favorite stories my mom tells about me took place when I was in kindergarten. I had only been there for a few days, and she came to pick me up from school. She was walking up to the playground to get me, and we made eye contact. I knew that this meant it was time to go home, so I went over to the little boy I was playing with and kissed him good-bye on the cheek. Then I ran to my mom, and we walked together back to our car. With more than a little shock in her tone, she asked, "Danielle, who was that little boy you just kissed?"

"Oh, that's Justin. He's my boyfriend now," I replied confidently.

"No, you do not have a boyfriend, because you are five," my mom replied. "Let's not kiss any boys until you're ready to start dating—in ten years, OK, Danielle?"

Ben and me lost in conversation (and dance) at my thirteenth birthday party.

Obviously, we had no idea what was in store for my future, but I listened to my mom and didn't kiss another boy until I was twelve. That boy happened to be Ben Savage, whom I am lucky enough to call my TV husband on the Disney Channel show *Girl Meets World*. Like most twelve-year-olds, I was nowhere near ready to start dating, but Cory and Topanga, our characters on *Boy Meets World*, were a little more advanced than I was.

In August 1993, I started my first week playing the character of Topanga Lawrence on *BMW*—more than twenty years ago, which is hard for me to believe. That episode focused on Cory not wanting to stand out from the rest of his peers; he believed it would be easier to go through life if he blended in with everyone else. Topanga, the self-confident, totally secure flower child that she was, tried to tell Cory that it was better to be true to himself because that was what made him unique. At the very end of the episode, Cory proved that he had learned this valuable lesson, and in response, Topanga kissed Cory against the middle school lockers.

Throughout the week of rehearsal, Ben and I never actually kissed. We'd rehearse the scene until it was time for *the kiss*, and then we'd just pretend. We never discussed if we were nervous or if we had ever kissed another person before. We just rehearsed all week, in complete denial of what was to come, and moved along. Five days later, it was tape day. Our one-hundred-fifty-person crew, four cameras, writers, producers, ABC executives, and three-hundred-person live studio audience were all about to witness my first kiss. Oh, did I mention our families were there, too? My mom, dad, brother, and grandparents were all in attendance to watch me film my first *BMW* episode—and, therefore, watch me kiss Ben Savage. As you can imagine, I got nervous.

"Ben," I said quietly. "Have you ever kissed a girl before?"

"Why? Have you ever kissed a boy before?" he asked me in a whisper.

"No, and I'm getting nervous now," I told him.

He smiled at me and said, "I'm a little nervous, too, but don't worry. We'll be fine." My nerves were instantly calmed. Ben has always had that effect on me.

Five minutes later, it was time to start the scene. I looked over at Ben, and he had gone completely white. We were both so incredibly anxious, and he wouldn't even look at me. Our director pulled us around the corner and away from everyone else's view.

"Ben, Danielle, I know this is probably awkward for you, but I really need you to commit to the kiss. Don't pull away too fast. If you can do it right, we won't have to do it many times," he said.

Ben and I looked at each other and nodded. We were standing right next to each other and could feel each other shaking, but we had to start the scene. We kissed, and the studio audience went crazy. Miraculously, we didn't pass out. Even though nothing went wrong on the first take, we still ended up doing the scene at least five times, and every time we kissed, our nerves lessened. It was a good thing, too, because we went on to kiss almost every week for the next seven years.

During the first few years of high school, I had a couple of not-so-serious boyfriends. I was once asked out by a cute guy from school whom I didn't know very well. He wanted to take me to the Coffee Bean & Tea Leaf after school, and my mom said I could go if she met him first. He came to pick me up, and while my mom was talking to him at the door, he casually mentioned that his only goal in life was to live at the beach. My mom told him that he'd better plan to have a good job, because beach houses were expensive.

He replied, "Oh, I don't care if I have a house. I'm OK with being a bum as long as I have a surfboard and forty bucks a week to eat."

My mom smiled and made it clear that the conversation was over. She patted me on the back and sarcastically said, "Sounds like you got a good one."

We had a completely uninteresting coffee date, and I avoided him at school until he graduated.

Next, I went out with a guy who only had one word in his vocabulary: *dude*. Every story started and ended with *dude*. One day, he came over to my parents' house and wanted to play a game where he would trace a word on my back and I had to guess what that word was. He traced a word on my back, and before I could even say what I thought it was, my mom yelled from the other room, "*Dude*. I can guarantee the word he traced was *dude*." She was correct.

I didn't have my first serious boyfriend until I was a junior in high school. His name was Jason, and although he didn't go to my school, he lived pretty close to me. We spent most of our free time together: going to dinner with our families, shopping, seeing movies, and making each other laugh. I was crazy about him, and after we had been together for a little more than six months, we decided we wanted to lose our virginity to each other. Because my mom and I had always been so close and had such an honest relationship, I thought it would be a good idea to share this piece of news with her over lunch.

"Mom, remember when you had the 'sex talk' with me years ago?"

"Of course. Where is this headed?" she asked while struggling to swallow a bite of her salad.

"Well, as you know, Jason and I are in love. Valentine's Day is coming up, and we have decided to lose our virginity that night," I said, desperately trying to avoid eye contact with her.

She put her fork down and looked me square in the eyes. "Danielle, I do not think that is a good idea. You know that I think Jason is wonderful, but you guys have not been together that long in the scheme of things," she pleaded.

"Uh, hello? We've been together for *six months*!" I whined.

"Six months is nothing. It isn't even the length of one whole school year! And what does Valentine's Day have to do with anything?" she asked.

"Well, we thought that it would be extra-romantic if we lost our virginity on Valentine's Day," I explained.

"Valentine's Day is a fake holiday created by card companies, Danielle. No matter when you lose your virginity, it is going to be special. You don't need a nonsense holiday to do that for you. Listen, I know you are going to lose your virginity at some time, but do me a favor and just think about what I've said. I really think you'll be making a big mistake if you don't," she concluded.

I agreed to think about what she'd said, and my mom and I continued our lunch without any awkwardness. I was happy that I'd decided to talk to her about this important moment in my life, and I was extremely thankful that I had a mom I could be so open with. I thought a lot about what she'd said and decided that she was right; I wasn't ready, and our relationship hadn't shown the test of time yet. Sure enough, Jason and I broke up a few months after Valentine's Day. Sometimes moms give the best advice.

After Jason, my next serious boyfriend was Lance Bass. It was 1998, and boy bands, namely *NSYNC and the Backstreet Boys, were all the rage. ABC was going to air two hours of its "TGIF" programming live, and they asked me to cohost the event. One of the producers of the telecast told me that they wanted to get a boy band to perform in between the shows and asked if I had a preference between *NSYNC and the Backstreet Boys. Without hesitation, I told her it had to be *NSYNC.

A few months later, the night of the live telecast arrived. Sure enough, ABC had booked *NSYNC for the night, and I got to meet all of the guys. Every single one of them was so incredibly nice and excited to be there. Justin, Lance, and I began talking and realized we were all pretty close in age. For the rest of the night, the three of us joked and laughed and had a good time. It was one of the most fun work events I've ever done.

At the end of the night, Chris, Joey, JC, Justin, and Lance all went backstage to change out of their show clothes before they had to get back on their tour bus. Sad that I didn't even get to say good-bye to them, I started walking outside to my car.

"Danielle!" Lance called from inside the venue.

"Yes?" I said.

"Um, is there any way that I could get your phone number?" he asked nervously while handing me a piece of paper and a pen.

"Sure," I said, and I wrote my number down. "It was really nice to meet you."

"Thanks! You, too," he yelled as he went running back inside to finish changing.

I walked back to my car with a huge smile on my face. He was so cute and so funny and so incredibly kind. *I'd be a lucky girl if he called me*, I thought to myself. And I was right.

A few days went by, and I didn't hear from Lance. Then, one night after dinner, my phone rang. It was a number I didn't recognize, but, hoping it was him, I answered anyway.

"Danielle?" this incredibly deep voice said.

"Yeah," I muttered.

"This is Lanston. I had a nice time with you—hey! Hey!"

"Uhhh, Lance?" I laughed.

Suddenly, the voice was different. Deep but not quite as booming.

"Danielle? Oh, my gosh. I'm so sorry. This is Lance, but that was Justin pretending to be me a second ago."

I started laughing as Justin yelled into the phone, "Danielle, I only did that because he's been too nervous to call you!"

Lance told him to shut up, and we started a conversation. We ended up talking for four hours that night—and Justin only chimed in with embarrassing Lance stories about a hundred times.

During the next few weeks, Lance and I talked on the phone almost every single night. He was on tour, and I was working on *Boy Meets World*, but every day, I looked forward to coming home and receiving a phone call from him. Toward the end of the year, he had a few days off and asked if he could fly to LA to visit me. I hadn't even seen him since we met a few months earlier, so I was understandably very excited about that idea. I asked my mom if Lance could stay with us for a few days. She told me that she would talk to my dad about it, but she was OK with the idea as long as we were all in agreement that he would stay in the downstairs bedroom and I would stay in my upstairs bedroom—absolutely no sneaking around after my parents went to bed. I told her that was perfectly acceptable and asked her please to talk to my dad ASAP.

The next day, my mom broke the news to me that my dad had said, unequivocally, no. I was heartbroken and begged her to talk to him again, and like the wonderful mom she is, she did. That night at dinner, my parents told me they had decided that since Lance spent so much of his time on the road, staying in hotels, they wanted him to feel at home if he was going to come visit me. They told me that I was seventeen and had never done anything that broke their trust, so they were going to give me the benefit of the doubt and let Lance stay at our home. I was so excited and asked if I could be excused from dinner to call Lance and tell him.

A couple of weeks later, Lance arrived. It was a little awkward at first. We were both nervous, and even though we had spent months talking on the phone for hours every night, we hadn't been face-to-face since the day we met. Lance told me we were going on our first date that night and that I should dress up in something appropriate for Christmas—even though it was only October. Lance and I retired to our separate rooms and got ready. I had no idea where we were going, but I was excited.

An hour later, Lance and I met downstairs for our date.

"Where are we going?" I asked.

"We are going to watch Celine Dion film her Christmas special *These Are Special Times!*" he exclaimed.

Now, I love me some Celine Dion, but perhaps that should have been my first sign that he was gay? I was apparently blinded by "The Power of Love"—my pun game is on point!

During the next few months, Lance and I were able to spend much more time together. He was working in LA more often, and I went to Mississippi for a few days before Christmas to meet his wonderful family. It wasn't always easy to date Lance. All of the *NSYNC guys had serious girlfriends—including Chris's girlfriend, Danielle, who became one of my greatest friends and was a bridesmaid in my wedding—but their management wouldn't allow them to talk publicly about their relationships. *NSYNC was experiencing major success, and girls all over the world wanted to believe that they had a chance to date Justin, JC, Joey, Chris, or Lance—and publicly acknowledging a girlfriend would instantly crush those dreams. I imagine dating a member of *NSYNC was very similar to dating one of the Beatles during their heyday—absolute pandemonium everywhere they went.

Luckily for us girlfriends, all of the guys were able to be in LA for Valentine's Day. They had just come off a European tour, and they enlisted the help of a very good friend, Sarah, to help them plan a romantic day for their lady loves. Lance came to pick me up very early in the morning on February 14. He didn't tell me what he had planned but said that I should wear pants. (Until now, I

Young love: Lance and me in LA.

never realized how much of our relationship Lance spent telling me what to wear. Oh, how I miss his fashion advice!)

The first activity he had planned was horseback riding in the mountains. We had a great time, and I was so happy he'd told me to wear pants. We were riding without saddles, and both of us were drenched in horse sweat—hot, right? Wrong. Lance took me home so I could shower and told me to meet him back at his hotel at six P.M. so he could take me to dinner. Unfortunately, Lance didn't tell me what the dress code was this time. I have no memory of what I wore, so I'm sure it was some craptastic outfit.

We went to a romantic dinner. We talked about our relationship, all six months of it, and how much fun we had together. I decided that night that Lance was the man I wanted to marry. He was a perfect boyfriend: he was incredibly kind, funny, loyal, smart, and successful, and he had a great family. I knew it would be hard to do better than Lance, so my mind was made up; we were going to get married within the next two years. Did it ever occur to me that I should make sure Lance was OK with this plan? Absolutely not. My mind was made up.

After dinner, we went back to his hotel. At Lance's request, Sarah had come in while we were at dinner and lit the fireplace for us. There was a humongous bouquet of two dozen long-stemmed red roses on the table and rose petals sprinkled from the couch and up the two stairs that led to the king-size bed. My stomach was full of butterflies, and I wasn't sure what to do, so I went and sat down on the couch. Lance told me he had a pres-

Lance decided on a casual look for our wedding. Kidding!
This is us on the Boy Meets World set the day Cory and
Topanga got married.

ent for me, and he came out from the bedroom with a huge box. I pulled off the lid, and there were at least fifteen items inside. They were all gifts that pertained to me or our relationship: a Barbie nightgown because he knew about the Mattel commercials in my past, a book about Taurus birthdays because he was born May 4 and I was born May 5, a Prada makeup bag that he bought in Italy, and so on. OK, that last one didn't have anything to do with me or our relationship; it was just sweet that he thought of me while he was in Italy.

After I had thoroughly looked through all of my gifts, Lance asked if I wanted to listen to music. We walked up the stairs to the bedroom, turned on the radio, and "You're Still the One" by Shania Twain was playing. I silently decided that it would be our first dance song at our wedding.

In June of my senior year Lance was going to be in Japan, which meant he would have to miss my prom. Being the loyal girlfriend that I was, I decided not to go without him. Unbeknownst to me, the *NSYNC travel schedule changed at the last minute, and he found out that he would be able to make it. Instead of just calling to tell me the good news, he sent Sarah over to my house with a dozen long-stemmed red roses that had a note attached: *Will you go to prom with me? Check yes or no.*

There were two little boxes under the message, one titled *yes* and the other titled *no*—just like the *Do you like me?* notes we wrote in elementary school. It was incredibly sweet, so I obviously checked the *no* box and called him a jerk (not really).

Lance and I had an amazing time at prom. He enjoyed dancing, he didn't get upset when classmates asked to take pictures with him, and he didn't try any funny business at the hotel afterward—a father's dream prom date for his daughter.

About a month after prom, I moved out of my parents' house and moved in with Danielle. One afternoon, Lance called and broke up with me over the phone. He was vague about why he didn't want to be with me anymore but basically just told me that our schedules were too different and he didn't have the time

*Lance and me in my parents' front yard
before we left for prom.*

or the energy to be a good boyfriend. I tried to tell him that he was a fantastic boyfriend and that even though he had a hectic travel schedule, I felt we had made a solid effort to see each other whenever we could. My attempts were in vain, and at the end of the phone call, I was single and in tears.

I called my mom to tell her what happened and expected her to be shocked and disappointed. Turned out that while she was sad for me and didn't want to see me unhappy, she wasn't at all shocked.

MOM: Danielle, can I ask you a question?

ME: Of course.

MOM: Do you think there's any possibility that Lance is gay?

ME: What? No!

MOM: Danielle, I think Lance was a wonderful boyfriend, and he was always good to you, but I think he might be gay.

Lance and I remained friends, and a few years after we broke up, he came out privately to his friends, including me. I never once felt anything but happiness for him. I didn't feel lied to or betrayed; I could only imagine how hard it must have been for him to be in one of the most adored boy bands of all time, an object of desire for women all over the world, and to be afraid that if people knew he was gay, it could all go away in a heart-beat. I knew coming out was a major step for Lance and would help make him feel happy, whole, authentic, and honest, and I just wanted to love and support him in any way I could. I'm proud that Lance and I are still friends—and he is still one of the best boyfriends I have ever had.

In 2007, after a couple of failed long-term relationships, I decided to try out this thing I had heard of called dating. I had never been good at dating. I always got emotionally invested in the first person I went out with after a breakup and ended up in another dead-end relationship. This time, I was determined to keep my options open and find someone I could really count on.

While visiting friends in New York, I met a nice guy named Stan at a mutual friend's birthday party and we had a short but very nice conversation. (In this chapter, the names of Stan and Mike have been changed, because I'm not a total jerk—only eighty percent jerk.)

At the time, I was in the middle of planning a bachelorette party for one of my best friends, Brandy, and I told Stan that we were planning to go to Las Vegas. He kindly told me that he owned a home in Vegas and said that if we wanted to go to any clubs while we were there, he could get us a table. I let him know that I appreciated his offer but that none of us was all that into the club scene.

About a month later, I received a call from Stan, who had gotten my number from our mutual friend. He asked how my bachelorette-party planning was going and if there was anything he could do to help. I didn't need his assistance, but we ended up talking on the phone for more than an hour. He was really talkative and funny and seemed totally sincere. I couldn't really remember what he looked like, because the only time we'd met, it was late at night and dark, but that didn't really matter much to me. I had never been one to be attracted to someone strictly because of his looks, so I decided to keep in touch with Stan and see where things went.

For the next few months, we continued to talk on the phone a couple of times a week. I learned quite a bit about Stan: he loved traveling, eating, and staying busy; he owned a house in Brooklyn and worked in Manhattan as a senior manager at a private jet company, where he had a nice corner office; he had a young son he was absolutely crazy about and, despite their breakup, had a good relationship with his son's mother; he used to be a stock broker before he decided to invest all of the money he made into restaurants and bars in New York and Vegas. He was also very generous. He said his mother was currently living with him and his son, because she was lonely and loved spending time with them. He also owned three cars: a Lincoln Navigator, a Jeep Cherokee, and a Cadillac Escalade. When I asked why anyone who lived in New York needed three cars, he said that he drove one to work and the other two were "for friends and family who came to town." Jeez. I thought I was being nice by giving my guests a clean pillow when they came to visit.

Even though Stan wasn't shy about talking about expensive things he intended to buy (he once told me he was thinking of buying a beach house for himself as a birthday present—who does that?), he didn't come across as pretentious. That would have been an immediate turn-off.

After a few months of talking on the phone and texting regularly, I got the opportunity to go to New York for work. I called

Stan to tell him the good news, and he was very excited. We made plans to spend my first day in New York together, and he said he would plan us a fun afternoon date. He also offered to pick me up at the airport, so I gave him my flight information and told him to meet me at baggage claim. I spent at least an hour trying to figure out what I should wear on the plane. I wanted to be comfortable for the five-and-a-half-hour flight but also look cute when he picked me up. I decided on a great pair of jeans, a cute top, and a pair of knee-high boots. I've never called myself particularly creative.

When my plane landed, I made my way to baggage claim and picked up my bag. I texted Stan to see if he was already at the airport, and he said he was running about thirty minutes late. I wasn't particularly pleased with that, because I am insane about time management—if I'm not fifteen minutes early somewhere, I feel like I'm late. But I reminded myself that just because *I* was crazy about being on time, that didn't mean everyone else was, and I shouldn't let it bother me.

What did bother me was what happened next.

I was waiting for Stan on the curb in my boring but perfectly adorable outfit when he pulled up next to me in his Jeep. All of his windows were down, and he was blasting techno music at a level that could burst eardrums. I was completely mortified. Every person in sight was staring at us, all shaking their heads at the inconsiderate level of his music. He jumped out of the car to help me with my bags, and I noticed that he was wearing a *tank top*. Apparently, I was overdressed for our first official date.

As we drove off from the airport, I started looking around his car—it was filthy. There was trash all over the floor in both the front and back, and there was a thick layer of dust over the dashboard. I decided it was best for me not to pay too much attention to the details of his car and instead focus on Stan. I tried to ask him how his day had been, but conversation was hard, because he still hadn't turned down the volume of his music. My head was hurting. I yelled at the top of my lungs, "Do you mind if I turn this down?" and he nodded that it would be acceptable.

STAN: What's wrong? You don't like techno music?

ME: No, it's not that. I'm just happy to finally be able to talk to you in person, but I couldn't hear you over that volume.

STAN: Oh, yeah. Sorry. I drive with the radio like that all the time, so it doesn't sound that loud to me.

Call me crazy, but don't people grow out of driving around blasting music with their windows down at, like, seventeen? Stan was twenty-eight.

Before we could begin our date, I wanted to stop at my friend Julie's apartment, because I was going to be staying with her while I was in New York and I wanted them to meet. When we got to Julie's apartment, I introduced Stan and Julie and excused myself to take a quick shower.

When I came out of the shower, Julie and Stan were sitting in the living room in silence, and Julie had a big smile on her face. *That must have gone well*, I thought to myself. Stan asked if I was ready to leave for the day, and I said I was.

We left Julie's apartment and started walking.

ME: So! What are we doing today?

STAN: Whatever you want, babe. The world is our oyster!

He threw his arms in the air. It was at this point that I was fairly certain that I was taller than Stan (I'm five foot one). I also spotted his gold tooth. His. Gold. Tooth. After a few discussions about what food we were in the mood for, we decided to go to a burger place near Julie's apartment.

STAN: How was your flight?

ME: It was fine. I was able to sleep, so it went by quickly.

STAN: Oh, good.

ME: Yeah . . . I always sleep on planes.

STAN: Looks like you brought the good weather with you!

Apparently, we were already out of conversation and were discussing the exciting topic of weather now.

After lunch, Stan asked if I wanted to stop by his work to see his office and meet some of his coworkers. I wasn't sure why he wanted to go to his office on a weekend but didn't want to decline his offer. Plus, I wanted to see the corner office he loved so much.

When we got there, I realized why he wanted to introduce me to everyone. He had apparently been telling his coworkers that he was taking "Topanga" out on a date, because no one there knew my real name. His corner office also turned out to be a cubicle that was surrounded by a hundred other cubicles just like it. I started to worry that everything about Stan had been too good to be true.

After we looked at his cubicle and took pictures with his coworkers, Stan asked if I wanted to "go hang out in a park." The way our in-person conversation had been going thus far, I was really hoping we could do an activity of some kind, but this was the date Stan had planned, supposedly, so I decided to go with the flow. He asked which park I wanted to go to, and I told him that since I didn't live there and was therefore not too familiar with any park other than Central Park, he should probably be the one to pick where we went. He decided on a small park a few blocks from his office, and we grabbed a couple of seats at a table.

STAN: Wow. I can't believe this weather.

ME: Yep. It is a nice day today.

Really? Back to the weather again? I tried to change the subject and asked him about a topic he loved: softball.

ME: Don't you have a softball tournament this week?

STAN: Yeah, it starts tonight. I'm so glad we're gonna have nice weather for it!

OK, this guy was way too into the weather. I told Stan that I was really tired and wanted to go back to Julie's to take a nap. He said he needed to get back home to get ready for softball but that he would call me later and we would set up another night to go to dinner while I was in town. I thanked him for picking me up at the airport, and we parted ways.

When I got back to Julie's apartment, she was anxious to hear how our date had gone. I told her what had happened, and she started laughing uncontrollably. Julie told me that she didn't want to forget the details of their conversation, so she had written an email to me and saved it in her draft folder. These were the contents of the email.

Danielle,
This is a detailed account of my painful conversation with Stan.

ME: So you have a house in Brooklyn? I work in Brooklyn.

STAN: Yep.

ME: Do you live by yourse—

STAN: YES!

ME: And Danielle says you're out in Vegas a lot?

STAN: Yeah, I have a huge place in Spanish Terrace [*no idea if that exists, and I might be wrong, but it was Spanish something*] but I'm taking over [*forget the company name*] so I'll basically be running forty percent of Vegas nightlife. So I'm gonna sell my place and just buy a sick, huge place, like five bedrooms, off the Strip.

ME: Oh . . . that's awesome. One of my best friends' bachelorette party is out there in July, but we don't really have an idea where we should go. The other times I've been, I haven't had to plan anything . . . [*Willing Stan to jump in!*]

STAN: [*Crickets . . .*]

I am now ready to kill you for taking more than forty-five seconds to get ready.

ME: So, if you have any suggestions, let me know.

STAN: OK. [*Crickets for about twenty seconds . . .*] You should go to Tryst one night.

I am officially dying. I get up to see what you were doing, and I hear that the shower is still running, so I go back to awkwardly entertain Stan.

ME: So you drive in for work? That must be nice to not have to deal with the trains in the morning.

You know, since he has three cars, two for "friends and family members."

STAN: No. I take the train. It's like an hour and twenty minutes to drive here usually. Even at night sometimes.

Danielle, this conversation is officially over. Where he lives in Brooklyn is a twenty-minute ride away, and I'm done talking to him.

I told Julie that the only thing that surprised me was that he didn't mention what nice weather New York was experiencing. I filled her in on the awkward encounter at work and about how we had nothing to talk about in person. She told me that I should give him one more opportunity while I was in town.

The next day, Stan called me and wanted to make dinner plans. I told him which nights I was free, and he told me he would have to check with his mom to see when she could babysit his son. I commented on how lucky he was that his mom could watch his son so he didn't need to worry about hiring a babysitter. He responded, "She's the best. That's the majority of the reason she asked us to move in here." Uh, what?

ME: Asked you to move in where? I thought *she* was living with *you*, not the other way around.

STAN: Yeah, yeah, that is what I meant. I meant that she asked me to buy this particular house because then she could live here, too.

ME: OK, because you kind of just made it sound like you live with your mother.

STAN: It's, like, both of our house.

Apparently, I was "dating" a pathological liar. This "senior manager" with a corner office worked in a cubicle and lived with his mother. The worst part about it was that had he just been honest with me, I wouldn't have blinked an eye. Sure, I would have preferred to date a twenty-eight-year-old man who had a place of his own, but he also had a young son. If Stan went through hard times and needed someone he trusted, like his mother, to help get his son to and from school and decided it made the most sense to move in with her, I wouldn't have thought twice about it. And I certainly couldn't have cared less about a corner office versus a cubicle. But the combination of Stan's lies and the fact that he incorrectly thought that I was the type of girl he needed to impress with phony material things was what turned me off for good. Men, lying to a woman you want to date is *never* a good idea, but there is also such a thing as *too much* honesty.

After my experience with Stan, I was feeling pretty discouraged, so I decided to allow my mom to set me up with a very handsome guy who worked with my dad. I had met Mike (not his real name) at one of the company Christmas parties, and we got along well. My mom asked if she could give him my phone number, and I told her she could. What followed next was a series of wonderful text and email exchanges between Mike and me. He was funny, smart, sweet, and handsome, and he had a good job; on paper, he was perfect. My parents were having a barbecue that Saturday, and I thought it might be a relaxing way for us to get to know each other, since he already knew my parents. Via text, I invited Mike to the barbecue, and he agreed to come—with one caveat. He wanted to take me on a proper date first, on Friday night. I told him I thought that sounded like a great idea.

When Friday night arrived, I realized that maybe this wasn't the best plan. What if we didn't have a good date? What if I decided we didn't have any potential? I couldn't exactly uninvite him to my parents' barbecue—that would be humiliating. I reminded myself that I didn't need to make a decision about our potential after the first date—it was OK just to go with the flow.

I met Mike at his house before dinner. He opened the door, gave me a hug, and complimented me on how I looked—one brownie point for Mike. He asked if I would like a tour of his place. His house was clean and decorated fairly well for a bachelor—one more brownie point for Mike. When we got to his bedroom, he said, "This is where the magic happens." Uh, gross—strike one for Mike.

Mike had picked a very nice steakhouse by the beach for dinner, and I was starving. We sat down, and our waiter brought over the wine list. Mike said, "Oh, thank God. I am so nervous—I need a drink immediately." He asked if I liked red wine, and I told him that I did, so he ordered a bottle. I started looking over the menu and asked Mike if he had any recommendations since this was one of his favorite restaurants and I had never been there.

MIKE: Everything is pretty good. I'm too nervous to eat, so I'm just going to have a side salad.

ME: You're just going to eat a *side salad*?

MIKE: Yeah, normally, I would order a steak, but I'm just too nervous to eat.

ME: OK, you've mentioned being nervous three times now. Why are you so nervous? I promise I'm not very scary.

MIKE: I don't know. After this wine, I'll probably feel better.

Now, call me crazy, but no one really wants to hear that her date needs to get intoxicated to make it through a meal with her. Strike two for Mike.

Our waiter came back to take our order, and Mike did indeed order a side salad. Without apology, I ordered an adult person's meal. Mike poured himself his third glass of wine while I was still on my first.

MIKE: I probably shouldn't tell you this, but I'm kind of drunk now, so here goes. I told a few friends that we were going to be eating here, and I asked them to show up and pretend that it was a coincidence—because I was really nervous.

ME: Uh, really? That seems a little weird, and I don't know why you're still so nervous, but OK.

Strike freaking three for Mike. He managed to finish his side salad without throwing up, and his friends never did "surprise" us. Mike asked if I wanted to take a walk since he wasn't quite ready to drive yet, and we left the restaurant. We walked around the beach for an hour, and his nerves seemed to have subsided. He was back to being the witty and sweet guy I had gotten to know via text and email, and I decided that before I made a judgment about him, I would see how the barbecue went the next day.

I went over to my parents' house early so I could fill my

mom in on how our date had gone. She was very optimistic that he would be much less nervous now that we had already hung out one-on-one. I was hopeful that she was right.

Mike arrived at my parents' house right on time, which I appreciated, because as I already told you, I am a nerd about time management. He gave my mom and me a hug hello and went into the backyard to say hello to my dad, who was managing the barbecue. After he was out there with my dad for fifteen minutes and never once looked in my general direction, I decided to join them outside. Mike and my dad were discussing basketball, and I tried to include myself in the conversation, but Mike wouldn't even make eye contact with me. I awkwardly stood next to him for a few minutes before heading back inside to see if my mom needed any help.

ME: Mom, did you see that? He won't even look at me.

MOM: Maybe he's nervous because he works with your dad and now he's at our house?

ME: Well, I guess that makes sense. Seriously, if this guy tells me he's nervous one more time . . .

After a couple of hours, Mike loosened up and we all had a good time. It came up in conversation that I was training for a half-marathon, and Mike perked up. He told me that he ran track in high school and running was one of his favorite things to do.

MIKE: Want to go for a run on the beach with me tomorrow?

ME: Well, I just started training, and I haven't done more than five miles at a time yet. Plus, I get bad shin splints, so I'm not very fast. I wouldn't be a good running partner for you.

MIKE: That's OK! We don't need to run fast or far.

ME: OK, let's go for a run tomorrow.

This had suddenly turned into a three-day date, and I wasn't sure how I had gotten myself into this situation.

The next day, I met Mike at his house before our run. We drove to his favorite part of the beach and stretched. We started running, and about a mile in, my shin splints started killing me. Mike was charging the mountain and running faster than I could ever dream of. He would run about a quarter of a mile ahead of me and then turn around and run back to me. This made me feel like a total loser, and I wasn't sure what was so fun about running with another person when you weren't anywhere near that person for half the time. Eventually, he got tired of my slow pace and started *pushing on my lower back with his hand,* urging me to run faster. It took everything in my power not to punch him in the face.

When we had run what I perceived to be three miles (it felt like a hundred miles), I told him I was done. Basically, I didn't want to play anymore, and I wanted to pack up my toys and leave. Mike asked if I wanted to get sushi for dinner, and I said that sounded nice.

When we were on our way to the sushi place, Mike told me that a few of his friends were at a taco shack down the street and he wanted to stop in and see them for a few minutes. I was a sweaty, disgusting mess and didn't feel like meeting anyone like that, but I didn't want to rain on his parade just because I wasn't at my most attractive.

When we got to the bar, it was three P.M., and his friends were drunk—and shirtless. One of them was covered in stickers and insisted on putting stickers all over my arms, and another was wearing a foam NASA helmet for some unknown reason. Long story short, Mike thought this was hilarious and didn't seem to be the least bit embarrassed about the fact that this was my first impression of them. After we hung out with them for about forty-five minutes, I told Mike I was getting hungry and we should go get sushi. I could tell he didn't really want to leave, but I was already starting to regret agreeing to get dinner with him, and I just wanted to get home.

Mike and I shared a semi-awkward dinner: neither of us really had too much to say, and I think we both realized we had not made a love connection.

Our bill arrived, and I pulled out my wallet and offered to pay, saying, "You got dinner Friday night."

"OK," Mike replied.

I was floored. Not in a million years did I think that he would take me up on my offer to buy dinner. This date had been his idea from start to finish, and it was only our second date, technically. Well, we never went out again—too many strikes for Mike.

CHAPTER 8

I HEART YOU WITH
ALL MY FART

I met my husband, Tim Belusko, at the end of 2008. It was my second semester in college, and we were in the same English class. Tim wasn't enrolled in the class, and he wasn't even on the wait list. He was simply trying his luck at getting into the class by showing up and hoping there would be an open slot.

This was a prerequisite English class, and on the first day, our teacher, Jim (great, Jim and Tim, this should be easy for you to follow; I'm going to make up a name for Jim—how about James? See how clever I am?), made it clear that he was a bit of a hard-ass (even though he encouraged us to call him Jim . . . er, James).

With a student in every seat and fifteen more students standing along the wall hoping to add the class to their schedules, James told us that he was going to be tough on us. This class required loads of writing—good writing—and he predicted that by the end of the semester, only a fifth of us would be left sitting in the seats. The rest would have failed out or simply dropped the class because it was too difficult. I have to admit, even though I was strong in English and a decent writer, I was nervous. I wasn't the only one, apparently. At least ten people got up from their seats and left the room, having decided they would try their luck next semester with an "easier" teacher. James was scary!

We were in a fairly big classroom, and after James filled the previously empty seats with all of the students who were on the wait list, he still had two seats available. He told the seven remaining students who were trying to add the class that they could put their names into a hat and he would draw two names. Those two lucky students would win the remaining empty seats. The first name drawn was not Tim. The second name drawn was not Tim. But then something hilarious happened. The student whose name was drawn second had a look of sheer horror on his face. Suddenly, he said, "Nah, man. I don't think I want to take this class with you." Then he ran out. Literally ran out. I mean, James was scary, but he wasn't wielding a machete or anything.

James and the rest of the class laughed as that terrified kid charged out of the room like he had a case of explosive diarrhea. James half-jokingly asked if anyone else wanted to bolt before he drew yet another name for the last remaining seat. Truthfully, I thought we all did, but no one else had the guts. Plus, I was sitting in the back and didn't want to trample the students in front of me, so I was actually kind of a hero for staying. I am still waiting for a few thank-you notes from students, for your information.

James reached his hand into the hat and pulled out another name. Tim. The student standing right next to James said "Yes!" and pumped his fist like Tiger Woods. *Hmm. That must be Tim,* I thought to myself. I told you I are smart.

Over the next few weeks in class, I developed a totally innocent yet completely creepy crush on this Tim fellow. He always sat in the front of the class, and I always sat in the back—in the only seat where I could still see his face. He was funny. He raised his hand to answer questions, and he always delivered the answers in a way that made the class chuckle. James seemed to like him, too. For about seven weeks, I never said a word to Tim, and he never said a word to me. Occasionally, he would glance back at me and we'd make eye contact, but then we'd both look off into the sky, pretending we were just thinking, and use our fingers to count, à la *Superbad*. This was extra-weird because we were in an English class and there was nothing to count.

Tim was handsome and clearly worked out. He wore white T-shirts that were one size too small, and absolutely no one was complaining. OK, I don't know what anyone else was thinking, but I wasn't complaining, and since I'm a total narcissist, I'm going to assume everyone shared my thoughts. He also had the *Mortal Kombat* dragon tattooed on the back of his calf. Tattoos aren't my thing, generally; I have two of my own that I already regret, so it's not like a guy with tattoos automatically makes me quiver. But I thought his was sexy, and I particularly liked the back-of-the-calf placement. I made a mental note to mention it to him if I ever introduced myself. Then I made a mental note not to introduce myself, because tattoo stories are boring even when they're of a cool video-game dragon. Finally, I made a mental note to stop taking stupid mental notes.

One day, during a small break from this ridiculously long class, I overheard/eavesdropped Tim talking about how poorly he was doing in his math class. He hated math, he couldn't understand his teacher, and he was worried that he wouldn't pass the class. Then he'd be stuck taking the same class again next semester. He did not seem happy about this, naturally.

I have always loved math, but when I went back to school at age twenty-seven, I hadn't been in a math class for nearly ten years. I took my placement exams and placed between Algebra I and Algebra II. Because what I had retained since high school placed me directly between the two math classes, the school let me choose which one I wanted to be in. I chose Algebra I, because I was afraid I wouldn't remember anything and spend my first semester in school failing math. *No bueno.* Clearly, my Spanish was still perfect, though.

The easy math class was a good choice for me, because I kicked butt in it. Remember Dr. H, whom I mentioned earlier? She taught me Algebra I, and I got one hundred percent on my first test and maintained that grade the whole semester. Dr. H had set me up perfectly to do well in Algebra II, which I was excelling in at the time.

When I heard Tim complaining about not passing, I spoke up. "What math are you in?" Immediately, I wondered why I was saying anything. What was I going to say if he was in some super-hard math class that I knew nothing about? *Oh, cool. I'm in Algebra.* And what was I going to say if we were in the same math class? *Oh, wow. Sucks you're failing. I have a nearly perfect grade, so nee-ner nee-ner.* There was no good answer to the question I asked, so why did I even open my mouth?

Then Tim said, "Algebra Two. I know it shouldn't be that hard, but I suck at math."

Thank God, neither one of us was very bright! "Well, I'm in the same class and doing really well. If you want, I can tutor you," said the Danielle who apparently doesn't think before she speaks and thinks nothing of randomly agreeing to tutor strangers while also having no prior experience tutoring anyone in anything.

"Are you serious? That would be amazing. Let's exchange numbers," said the funny Tim with the hot dragon tattoo and too-small T-shirt.

We exchanged numbers and walked back into class. I prayed he would never call me. How was I going to tutor someone? Where was I going to tutor someone? Why hadn't I learned to keep this giant mouth closed yet?

He called the next morning. I hadn't saved his number in my phone, so I didn't know who was calling but answered anyway. "Hey, Danielle? It's Tim from English. I'm hoping you might have some time to tutor me between now and next week? I have a test and could really use the help before the exam."

Ah, crap. Here we go. "Hi! Sure. Sure. Um, I can do it this Thursday if that works for you? I can come to your house."

"No, no," Tim said. "You're doing me a favor, so I'll come to you. What's your address?"

Don't ask me why I didn't think to meet in the school library, where sane people agree to tutor strangers, but I did not. I quickly saved his number in my phone under the name "Tim From English."

He arrived (on time!) at my house on Thursday evening. We sat at my dining-room table with homework, pencils, books, and binders splayed everywhere. He was eager to learn, and I was a surprisingly natural tutor, with the exception of asking "Does that make sense?" after everything I explained. Oh, and the other exception of my profuse sweating. I keep my house cold. Really cold. Like sixty-five degrees cold. But for some reason, I felt like it was three hundred degrees, and I couldn't stop sweating. I kept saying, "Is it hot in here?" He looked at me like I was crazy, and I instantly knew he wished he had brought a sweater.

I started tutoring Tim two or three times a week for the next few weeks. Sometimes he'd pick up food and we'd eat dinner while we studied, or sometimes I'd make dinner. We started studying together for all of our subjects, even the ones we didn't share. It was fun, and we helped each other be better students. At this point, I had never mentioned outright what I did for a living, he had never asked, and I literally had no clue if he knew that I was an actor. He never mentioned it, which, frankly, I loved. I liked this guy, and I didn't want to keep spending time with him if his ulterior motive was to tell people he was hanging out with Topanga. I wanted him to like being with me for me.

One night in class, James broke us up into small groups to work on a project. All of our desks were huddled in different circles, and Tim and I were not in the same group.

From across the room, someone yelled, "Wait! You *are* Topanga? I thought you just looked like her!"

Apparently, that group had gotten off topic, and they were discussing me. I smiled and nodded my head, a few people giggled, but overall the room was quiet.

Suddenly, Tim said, "Awwwwwwkwarrrrrrrrd," and the whole room erupted with laughter. With his typical humor, Tim had made me feel comfortable, gave the class a good laugh, and let me know that he did know what I did for a living—but most important, he let me know that I was still just his math tutor. Topanga the math tutor.

Toward the very end of the semester, we started dating. We hung out with his friends and our families over winter break. One night after the start of the spring semester, we went to dinner and came back to my house to do homework. Tim hated having to do homework in college, but, in typical Danielle fashion, I insisted on it. I may have technically been done tutoring him, but really, I had just begun my quest to make him a superior student. It was the least evil "evil plan" known to man—I'd make a terrible villain. About thirty minutes after dinner, Tim started feeling weird. He kept complaining of chest pains and writhing in his chair. I asked him if he wanted to go to the emergency room, but he brushed that off and insisted he was fine. But I knew what was wrong with him.

Tim was always leaving my house at random times. We'd be working on a math problem, and suddenly he would be charging out the door with his books. I'm not an idiot. Well, I am, but no one is better at this game than girls. Ladies, how many times have you had the conversation with your friends about how hard it is to "use the bathroom" when your man is around? A billion trillion times, right? For being fairly smart animals, humans are some of the dumbest around. We know that every single living thing poops and occasionally has gas, but we refuse to let anyone know that *we* are included in that every-living-thing category. Girls don't poop, and neither did Tim. Well, he pooped, just not anywhere near me.

Finally, I told him it was probably just gas and it would go away. He laughed and said I was probably right. A few minutes later, he said he was going to the bathroom, and we all know just saying those words made him brave. Then he walked past the downstairs bathroom and up into the upstairs bathroom. Extra-brave! He was literally spelling it out for me that what might happen in the bathroom would most likely be heard if we were on the same floor. I was impressed. He came back down a little while later, not feeling much better. He continued to get up every few minutes, walk upstairs, and then come back down after being in the bathroom for a minute or two. After about ten trips up the stairs and no homework getting done, this happened.

ME: You know, if you're just having gas, you can stay down here. You don't need to keep going up upstairs.

TIM: Really? Feels a little weird to just stay here but thanks.

Loudest fart ever.

TIM: Ugh, I feel so much better.

ME: Yay?

So this comfortable, fart whenever and wherever you want relationship continued for the rest of our dating years. Well, it continued for Tim. He didn't even blame it on the dog, like a regular person.

After we got engaged, Tim and I decided that our first dance at the wedding would be to a Sam Cooke song, since we were both huge Sam Cooke fans. We just couldn't agree on which song it would be, so I came up with a great idea.

ME: Why don't we play both songs and dance to them right now? We'll pretend it's our first dance, honey!

TIM: OK. That sounds like a good idea.

We smiled at each other. I wrapped my arms around Tim's neck, and he placed his hands gently on the small of my back. This was one of those romantic moments that you realize usually only happens in movies. But it was really happening! I was slow-dancing with the man I wanted to spend the rest of my life with. We were alone and pretending to share our first dance as husband and wife. We were so in love, and life was perfect.

ME: Babe. Are you kidding me right now? Did you just fart?

TIM: Oh, yeah. Sorry. I think it smells, too.

ME: You *think* it smells? Do you not actually smell that? I think I'm going to vomit.

TIM: Hahahaha. Sorry! Hey, you told me I could fart in front of you years ago!

ME: Babe, the whole song is two minutes and forty-three seconds. You really can't *not fart* for three minutes?

We didn't make it thirty seconds into the song, because I had to run out of the room. The stench was so potent it followed me into the next room, and I couldn't get away. Tim was laughing

This is what a first dance looks like when no one is farting.

hysterically, and he tried to convince me that I was overreacting and it wasn't that bad. I eventually fell to the ground, completely overcome with laughter at the absurdity of the moment. Was my romantic movie-esque first-dance moment ruined by my knight with smelly gas? No. The truth is, the memory of this event is something that will always bring a smile to my face, and I wouldn't trade it, or Tim, for anything or anyone. Not even for a Ryan-Gosling-in-*The-Notebook* level of romance.

After the smell had dissipated, I came back into the family room and Tweeted my experience to thousands and thousands of people. I guess I'm an oversharer, but I was thrilled to see how many people had similar experiences with their significant others. Tim and I have told this story so many times, and you know what? During our real first dance at our actual wedding (to John Legend's "All of Me," because I couldn't hear a Sam Cooke song without thinking of farts), he kept his gas to himself for a whole four minutes, and I had my romantic movie-esque first-dance moment with Tim From English in front of two hundred fifty people.

It was way more magical than the night he farted me out of the room, but it doesn't make me laugh as much when I think about it.

Tim is still saved in my phone as Tim From English (with one important addition).

CHAPTER 9

I DO ... WANT TO
SCREAM AT EVERYONE

When I first started writing this chapter, I was actively planning my wedding, and truthfully, I didn't know if I was going to have enough "crazy wedding stories" to fill it up and make it worthy of your time. I wonder when I'll stop being so naive.

Tim and I got engaged in May 2012, and I started planning our October 19, 2013, wedding a year in advance. We selected a venue, a date, and a wedding planner, then nothing too substantial happened for a few months. My mom and I didn't get into any blowup fights, Tim and I agreed on almost every aesthetic detail we envisioned (and when we didn't, he was smart enough to tell me he was probably wrong and I should just go with my instinct), and I thoroughly loved every second of prepping for one of the biggest days of my life. While it was all interesting to *me*, it must have been horrendously boring for others to hear about. Come to think of it, that's probably true of all wedding-planning stories; it's a pretty self-absorbed topic. So without further ado, here's mine!

Like a lot of modern engaged couples, we decided to create a wedding website. We had quite a few people traveling from all over the country to attend, and I wanted an easily accessible place for them to find all of the pertinent wedding info—hotel accommodations, venue address, time of the wedding, and so on. It turned out that the hardest thing about creating a wedding website was coming up with our own personal web address. I tried every easy-to-remember combination of our names and ended up being stuck with www.weddingwire.com/TandD2013. Not great, but it worked. And I'll be damned if it wasn't just the cutest little wedding website I had ever seen! (I told you this whole process was "me, me, me.")

After choosing the flowers, cake flavors, chairs, officiant, linens, tableware, lighting, and DJ, I sent out our invitations. One of the inserts was an information card where I asked everyone to visit our wedding website for any questions they might have regarding the wedding.

A week after I mailed all one hundred fifty invitations, my aunt called me. "Danielle," she said, "Auntie Dorothy tried to go to your wedding website to look at the hotel information, and the website said it didn't recognize that web address."

Ugh, doesn't anyone know how to use a computer? I thought to myself. Then I went and tried to visit our website myself. "This is not a valid web address," my computer monitor told me. I tried to reach someone at the Wedding Wire website and couldn't find any way of contacting them. I read their FAQ page. Nothing helped. I tried in vain to get to the bottom of who had screwed this up. There would be hell to pay! (Notice that not *once* did I think that *I* could have possibly been at fault here.)

For two whole days, I was a maniac about the stupid website. At four A.M. on what would have been the start of Wedding Website Mania: Day 3, I woke up in a panic. Was it possible that I had put the wrong web address on the invitations? *Noooo.* I had been so organized, so thorough, so together this whole time! I would *never* have made such a stupid mistake. I ran downstairs and looked at our Save the Date. It said www.weddingwire.com /TandD2013. Good. I grabbed one of our extra invitations and pulled out the info card: www.weddingwire.com/TandD. What had I done? After three straight minutes of Bridezilla yelling, I calmed down and called everyone who had been allowed to create a guest list: Tim, Tim's parents, my mom, and my dad. I told them what had happened and that they all needed to email everyone on their lists to explain what happened and give them the correct website address. They complied, and I emailed this message to everyone on my list:

> Subject: *Because no wedding is complete . . .*
> Body: *. . . without at least one disaster! :)*
>
> *Hello, nearest and dearest friends and family.*
> *Today I realized that I made a horrible mistake and*

*included the incorrect wedding website address on our
invitations! YIKES.*

*The correct website is: www.weddingwire.com
/TandD2013.*

Love,

Your frazzled bride

Almost all of our invited guests received the email and were
eventually able to view our website. Disaster averted. But boy,
how I wish that was my only disaster.

Two months before our wedding, my hairdresser quit working at the salon I had been going to for years. This was not
ideal, but I wasn't overly concerned. I have never been good
about getting my hair cut or colored on a regular basis. I usually
get two haircuts a year and every now and then decide I want
to add highlights or lowlights, depending on the time of year.
There are few things that can give you more self-confidence
than taking care of yourself, but the amount of time and energy
it takes to get regular haircuts, maintain a flawless manicure
and pedicure, exercise religiously, and eat five servings of fruit
and vegetables a day is exhausting. For most of us, something
has to give, and for me, that thing is hair upkeep. And working
out religiously. And eating five servings of fruits and vegetables.
Basically, I'm only good about getting my nails done on a regular basis.

Obviously, I knew I should get my lazy butt into the salon

Hair photo: Before

before my wedding, but I didn't want to try anything too far out of my norm. As any former bride will tell you, *right before your wedding* is not the time to try that new bob you thought you'd always love, the awesome new spray tan that just hit the market, or that antiaging laser skin peel you've heard about from all of your mom's friends. I just wanted to freshen up my layers, trim any dead ends, and even out my color.

As you can see from the photo of what my hair looked like before I went to the salon, my color was a little grown out. Two years before this photo was taken, I decided I wanted to try ombré hair. I loved it but hadn't touched the color since I had it done, and that wasn't the way I wanted my hair to look in our upcoming wedding photos. I went to the hair salon, talked with the new hairdresser, and told him what I wanted.

These were my exact words: "I'm getting married in a month, so I'm not looking to do anything drastic. I just want to add some more layers, cut off the dead ends, and even out my color. I want all of my hair to be the color that falls in between the lightest color on the bottom and the darkest color on the top."

His exact words to me: "So, you want it to look natural?"

"*Yes,*" I replied.

Then, in photo order, this is what happened.

Hair photo 1

Hair photo 1: He put a million foils on my head, and I wasn't sure what was happening. He told me he had been doing hair for close to thirty years. I could trust him, right?

Hair photo 2

Hair photo 2: This is an awful picture, but I think my face adequately describes what I was feeling when I got into the car. This photo was taken approximately half a second before I burst into hysterical tears and called my mom while having a full-blown panic attack.

Hair photo 3

Hair photo 3: This is a photo Tim took of me the next morning while my hair was in a clip. First of all, *cansomeonetellme-*

whatisnaturallookingaboutthis? Second, this is probably what I'll look like when I'm seventy-five years old.

Three days after that hair-color catastrophe, I went back to the salon and told the hairdresser that I absolutely hated my color. He agreed that it was not ideal (understatement of the year) and offered to correct it for me with toner and two different colors of lowlights. I was apprehensive about letting him near my head again, but I decided to trust him. I think I was just tired of wearing hats everywhere and waking up in the middle of the night crying about my Pepé Le Pew hair.

Thank goodness I trusted him. I left the salon looking and feeling a million times better, as you can see in the photo of my hair taken on our wedding day.

Hair photo: After

There are a lot of words women use to describe the way they want to look on their wedding day: *beautiful, elegant, timeless,* and *gorgeous. Seventy-five-year-old grandmother of six* is not on that list.

Another word not on that list: *fat.*

In December 2012, my former *Boy Meets World* castmate Rider Strong proposed to his girlfriend, Alexandra (Alex) Barreto. In mid-January, Tim and I had dinner with Rider and Alex at Will Friedle's house to celebrate our recent engagements and catch up on life (Ben Savage was, of course, invited, but he had previous plans that evening), as we have done several times over the years. Rider and Alex told us all about their engagement over dinner, and we shared many bottles of wine and laughs. I asked Rider when they intended to get married, and he said it would be before the end of 2013, but they hadn't selected a date or a venue yet. I said, "As long as it's not October 19, 2013, we're all good!" He laughed, and we both joked about how unlikely it would be for us to get married on the same weekend.

One month later, Tim and I were spending a glorious Saturday morning together golfing when I received a text from Rider.

> *Hi. Hope you guys are doing well. Alex and I found a venue we really love, and we want to be married there. The only weekend they have available is October 18–20, but then we remembered that might be your same wedding weekend?*

I immediately wrote back and said, *AH! Yes, it is. Please tell me you didn't already book it?*

Zero response from him after that. Tim and I continued our golf round, and I forgot about the text exchange. When I remembered it a few days later, I sent Rider another text.

Hey. Never heard back from you. Did you book that weekend for your wedding? I really hope not . . . we want to be at your wedding!

It took him a few more days, but he finally responded with *Yes. I'm so sorry. It was the only weekend they had available unless we wanted to wait until next year.*

Obviously, I love Rider like family. I absolutely adore Alex, and I was happy and excited for them to be taking this enormous step together. But selfishly, I was angry. I wasn't nearly as upset about the fact that he and Alex wouldn't be able to be at our wedding; I couldn't believe that I wouldn't be there to watch one of my favorite people say "I do" to the woman of his dreams. It pained me. But after I threw a short, private tantrum for Tim, I made peace with it in my mind like the mature woman I am/ try to be (most of the time). Of course, it was going to suck for Rider and me to get married on the same weekend, and of course, it was going to suck that our mutual *Boy Meets World* friends would have to choose between our two weddings, but at the end of the day, the most important thing was that we were both marrying the people we loved more than anything. That alone was beautiful and should make me feel happy, not sucky, so I celebrated for both of us from that moment on.

Even though Rider and I knew we were getting married on the same weekend, we didn't talk about it publicly. Rider is one of the most private people I know, so I never once thought that I should tell him to keep our wedding date(s) a secret; the idea that he would willingly tell press/Twitter/magazines the date he was getting married, much less tell anyone that he and I were getting married a day apart, literally never occurred to me. But that's exactly what he did.

I had been so good about keeping my wedding date a secret, and that was not easy for me. Where Rider is very private, I am much more of an open book. Every time someone asked me when I was getting married, I wanted to blurt out "October 19!" But I didn't. My go-to line was "Before the end of the year." Perfect, right? Completely truthful yet totally ambiguous, and that's the way I wanted it. We were getting married in downtown Los Angeles, a paparazzi minefield. I don't usually have a problem with paparazzi following me, because I don't go to many parties/clubs/famous restaurants (you can, however, find me in Red Robin regularly). Plus, I live fifty miles outside of LA and purposefully avoid areas that are well-known locations where celebrities and paparazzi hang out. If there was ever going to be a day when I didn't want to be called Topanga or have paparazzi snapping pictures of me, it was my wedding day.

Our wedding weekend arrived, and on the morning of October 18, I ran a load of dishes in the dishwasher, turned on the TV, and sat down on the couch with my morning coffee and my cell phone. That's my morning ritual; I love to simultaneously watch the news and read my Twitter feed to start my day. One of the first Tweets I read said, *Aw! Danielle and Rider are getting married on the same weekend?* Huh? What? How does this stranger on Twitter know this information? I kept scrolling through my feed until I saw a re-Tweet from an online magazine to which Rider had given a quote. He had confirmed that he was getting married that weekend and concluded with, *Bad news: Danielle Fishel's getting married this same weekend, so I'm missing some of my* Boy Meets World *family (that was my fault, she chose the date first).*

"Rider King Strong, what in the ever-loving H-E-double-hockey-sticks did you do?" I said to myself. You could tell I was mad because I used his middle name and an almost bad word. I calmly reminded myself that no one knew the exact location of my nuptials and that I probably didn't have anything to be concerned about.

I decided not to spend any more time worrying about it and to continue my busy morning. It was the day before my wedding, and I had a nail appointment at nine A.M. Then Tim and I were leaving for LA at noon, because we had our rehearsal dinner that night at a hotel right next to our wedding venue, Vibiana, which had previously been a stunning Catholic cathedral but was now a historic LA site for private events. Once we left the house, we wouldn't be returning home until after our Hawaiian honeymoon, so we had a *ton* of things to bring with us.

I stood up from the couch and walked barefoot through my kitchen so I could go upstairs to shower. I stepped in a puddle. "Dammit, Spike!" I said out loud. I assumed Spike had been a bad boy and peed on the floor, which, by the way, was totally likely. But then I looked down. The whole kitchen was covered in a half inch of water, but *of course* it was. Why wouldn't my dishwasher break for the first time the day I was leaving for *the biggest weekend of my life*? I went upstairs and grabbed five bath towels. I cleaned up all the water on the floor and texted Tim, who was at the gym for a pre-wedding-weekend workout.

> *Dishwasher broken. Water everywhere. Google "flooding dishwasher" when you get home, and please try to fix this while I get my nails done? Love you.*

I love Tim, but I honestly did not expect anything to be fixed when I got home. Tim has many talents, but being a plumber/handyman is not one of them. To be fair, I also don't possess those skills and have to ask my mom to come over and help me hang picture frames. But on this day, this crazy but about to be magical day, Tim managed to fix our flooding dishwasher! It was a wedding miracle. And my nails looked fabulous, and as we all know, that was way more important than any stupid dishwasher.

Tim and I loaded up the car and got on the road to LA. The rest of the day ran smoothly, and our wedding rehearsal and dinner went off without a hitch. My cousin's husband, also named Tim, was kind enough to take pictures for us.

As you can see, we basically made out the entire night. Our siblings looked really happy about it. I thought our rehearsal dinner was wonderful, but I had absolutely no idea what was in store for me the next day.

Because I love a few traditional wedding elements, Tim and I stayed in separate rooms the night before our wedding. My mom agreed to share a room with me, and when we woke up in the morning, I felt fantastic. I kept waiting for it to hit me that it was my actual wedding day, but it didn't until much later. I invited my bridesmaids over for breakfast and gave them their "thank you for spending tons of money and all of your time over the last year on me" gifts. A few minutes later, we made the short walk to the venue to have our hair and makeup done. Everyone looked so incredibly gorgeous, and when Tim and I saw each other for the first time, during our private first-look pictures, we both broke down in tears—it finally hit us that we were about to be husband and wife, and we were so full of joy.

To get inside Vibiana, all of our guests had to pass through gorgeous oversized black doors. One of the pictures on my "must-have photo list" was Tim and me standing alone outside with the large doors as our backdrop. Before we could take that picture, we needed to take our family photos. Directly opposite the large black doors at Vibiana's entrance was the altar where Tim and I would be saying "I do" later that day. I really wanted a photo with both our families, which wasn't very easy, since the Fishel crew alone rolls about forty deep. But since the altar had a few stairs, we figured that was a perfect place to gather and stack fifty people for a portrait.

When we finished taking what felt like 382 family pictures, I asked my photographer if we could go outside to take the picture of Tim and me in front of the doors at the entrance. She said, "I was just told we can't go out there because there are paparazzi everywhere." That news certainly didn't make me happy, but honestly, I was filled with so much joy that day that nothing was going to get me down. Plus, Vibiana was a private venue, and I had hired security, so I wasn't too worried about paparazzi sneaking onto the property. If not being able to take pictures in front of my favorite black doors because of paparazzi was going to be the worst thing to happen on my wedding day, I was *not* going to complain.

That actually *was* the worst thing to happen that day. I really don't have enough words in my vocabulary to properly describe to you what an otherworldly day our wedding day was. It was, hands down, the most spectacular, love-filled, joyful, peaceful, and fun day of our lives, to date. I refuse to believe that my wedding day was the best day of my life, because I believe that the best is always yet to come. However, it was definitely the best day I had ever experienced up to that point.

The morning after the wedding, Tim and I walked to breakfast with some friends who were in our wedding party. On our way, we stopped in front of Vibiana and took a picture, as husband and wife, in front of the large black doors I loved so much

but had been prohibited from taking pictures in front of the night before. We took one picture smiling at the camera and another one a second later where we were kissing.

We continued our walk to a local restaurant and had a great meal with our friends while we laughed and reminisced about the previous night. As the bride and groom, you don't really get to party at your own wedding. You spend most of your time making sure you've walked around and thanked everyone for coming, so it was fun to hear our friends' stories about their experiences—who drank too much, who spent the most time in the photo booth, who never left the dance floor. Overall, it was yet another near-perfect day.

After breakfast, our friends left us in Los Angeles and headed home. Tim and I called two of my best girlfriends, Julie and Kristy, who had flown in from New York for our wedding. They were staying at a hotel relatively close to ours, so we made plans to get together with them that night. Even though Tim and I were both exhausted, we didn't want to pass up another opportunity to see them. We didn't get to spend nearly enough time with them at the wedding, and our usual three-thousand-mile distance was currently only eight miles, so how on earth could we pass that up?

Tim and I had a drink in the lobby bar and headed up to our room to change. We had clothes, luggage, shoes, and makeup all over the place. OK, I had makeup all over the place. Tim doesn't (currently) wear makeup. We were leaving the next morning at 11:38 from Los Angeles International Airport to Maui, Hawaii, for our honeymoon, and I had arranged for a car to pick us up from our hotel at nine A.M. This time schedule allowed us a lot of extra time at the airport, but that's exactly how I like to travel/do everything in life: on time and without rushing. We weren't planning on getting home from Julie and Kristy's hotel too late, so we figured we had plenty of time to pack when we got home later that evening or, worst case, first thing the next morning.

We called a cab and met Julie and Kristy at their hotel at around eight P.M. They had ordered a bottle of champagne, which the four of us quickly consumed while sitting outside, next to the pool, in the relatively warm LA nighttime air. We quickly moved from champagne to vodka sodas, and then Tim noticed a ping-pong table. Julie, Kristy, Tim, and I are four of the most competitive people who roam this planet. I'm not kidding. We will compete over *anything*, even if that thing is an awful, no-good, very bad thing. We once got into a friendly but competitive argument over which one of us had previously been the meanest when drunk. That meant we started "bragging" about the times when we had been the most awful humans while intoxicated, because we all wanted to "win" that "competition." Nice, huh? (And don't ask me who won, because I'm not telling.)

Three rounds of vodka sodas later, it was ten thirty P.M., and we were loudly, and poorly, playing ping-pong. The hotel manager came outside and told us to keep it down, because guests were trying to sleep and we were being too loud. We apologized and tried to keep our voices down for about five minutes before we forgot all about the other guests and continued with our drinking and ping-pong shenanigans. At eleven thirty, we were kindly but firmly kicked out of the outside pool area.

At seven A.M., I woke up in bed and looked over my shoulder to find Tim. He wasn't there—but Julie and Kristy were. I realized Tim was sprawled across the bottom of the bed by our feet and immediately started laughing. He woke up within one second, and I whispered, "Babe, we need to go back to our hotel.

The car is going to be there in two hours, and we still need to pack and check out."

So there we were, newlyweds of less than forty-eight hours, doing a full-blown walk of shame from one Los Angeles hotel to another. I had mascara smudged under both my eyes, my head felt like it weighed eighty-five pounds, I was *starving*, and I had an incurable case of the giggles. Tim and I waited for our cab outside of Julie and Kristy's hotel—thank God, there were no paparazzi that morning, huh? Every time a car drove by, I envisioned the people driving past us thinking, *Look at those two losers! Ha! I bet it's so awkward because they barely know each other!* I desperately wanted everyone to know that I was walk-of-shaming *with my husband*, thank you. It's so much classier that way (it absolutely is not).

We got back to our hotel, showered, and packed our bags as quickly as we could. At 9:05 A.M., we hopped into our car and left for the airport. I hadn't been on Twitter or Instagram since the day before our wedding, and now that we had some time, I decided to post the picture we took in front of Vibiana the day before. Immediately after I posted it, I saw Tweets from a certain weekly gossip magazine that I won't name here. They had a photo of Tim, some family members, and me standing at the altar while we were taking family pictures before our wedding ceremony. It said, "See this exclusive shot of Danielle Fishel's wedding dress!" The picture was a paparazzi shot, supposedly taken from across the street, during one of the few seconds the double doors had opened to let in an elderly guest. Neither Tim nor I looked particularly good, because we were in the middle of intently listening to our photographer, whose back you could see in the photo. I was livid. I scrolled to the comments section to see what people were saying about the photo. I'm not really sure why I did that, to be honest. I know better than to check the comments section of any story, especially one about me, because 99.99 percent of the time, they are negative, hate-filled messages. I think I just felt violated knowing someone had stolen a moment from one of the most precious days of my life and wanted to see what the reaction was.

The first few comments consisted of things like "She really should have lost some weight for her wedding," or "She looks fat," or "They don't look very happy," or, my personal favorite, "People really need to work on their resting faces. They look miserable, especially that bitch for a bridesmaid." That "bitch for a bridesmaid" happened to be my amazingly sweet *sixteen*-year-old sister-in-law, and who on God's great earth works on their *resting face*? Was the person posting this comment a professional happy-resting-face-ologist? I don't think that job exists, but if it does and that is how you make a living, go screw yourself.

In some sort of furious, postwedding Bridezilla moment, I grabbed my phone and Tweeted: *Ppl saying I was FAT @ my wedding: u r the worst kind of ppl on the PLANET. I weigh 107 pounds & am 5'1". YOU are the reason anorexia exists.*

In hindsight, I have mixed emotions about whether I should have responded to the negativity at all. On one hand, bringing attention to negative people by calling them out on Twitter is usually not a good idea. That has a tendency to create more negativity, and in a sense, you've only opened yourself up for more judgment. People love to say that celebrities don't have a right to complain, because they chose a profession that puts them in the public eye and "that's why they make the big bucks." To an extent, that is true, and most of the time, I am really good about letting things roll off my back. I don't "feed the trolls," as they say. On the other hand, just because I am in the public eye, that doesn't mean that I no longer have the right to stand up for myself. I *despise* that we live in a culture where a woman's self-worth is determined by her appearance and weight. Let's say I was "fat" on my wedding day—what would that mean? Would that mean I wasn't entitled to wear a beautiful wedding dress and marry the man I love? Would that mean I was unlovable, incapable of giving love, and undeserving of a day to celebrate love with my closest friends and family?

Our society's obsession with women's weight makes me so angry. Think about the message this sends to young girls. On *Girl Meets World*, I play the mom of a twelve-year-old girl named Riley Matthews. In real life, I spend a lot of time on set with the girl who brings Riley to life, Rowan Blanchard. I also spend a lot of time with Sabrina Carpenter, who plays Riley's best friend, Maya. Despite the fact that I am not a mom to children of my own, these girls' names, faces, and minds popped into my head when I read that people believed I looked fat on my wedding day. I knew these two girls in particular, and maybe other young girls, looked up to me. I didn't want them to read the "she's so fat" comments online and then look at me and make a conscious or unconscious decision never to let themselves get that "fat." I am not a stick-thin model, and I never have been, but that is *perfectly OK.* Not only was I standing up for myself, but I truly felt like I was taking a stance on behalf of every young girl who looked up to me.

After I hit send on the Tweet, Tim looked at me and said, "You didn't say anything publicly, did you?"

"Of course I did," I said. "I just Tweeted about it."

He implored me to shut my phone off and not look at anything online for the rest of the day. He had a point. We were in a car on our way to the airport to leave for our honeymoon. What business did online comments from strangers have in this once-in-a-lifetime experience?

We got to the airport at 9:45 A.M., grabbed our bags, and went inside to check in. We handed the attendant our driver's licenses and discussed what we should do with the extra time we had before our flight took off. Tim was starving and wanted to eat, but I reminded him that we would get to eat on the plane, because we were flying first class. I love first class and am fortunate enough to get to fly that way when I travel for work. It's just too expensive for us normally, but my dad was generous enough to buy us first-class honeymoon tickets as a wedding present. I could not wait to get on that plane, cuddle up on Tim's shoulder, and have a glass of champagne.

After we had been standing at the counter for longer than it should normally take to check two people in for a flight, the attendant said, "Do you have your reservation number? I'm not showing a flight that leaves at eleven thirty-eight A.M." Oh, God. Tim and I looked at each other with wild eyes. *Please don't tell me I screwed this up, please don't tell me I screwed this up*, I kept repeating inside my head. I pulled out my phone and searched through my emails to find our reservation number. Right there, in an email from my dad, was our flight information.

"I thought our Maui *arrival* time was our *departure* time!" I frantically said out loud to no one in particular.

Tim looked at me and immediately burst out laughing. It took me three seconds to realize why he thought this was so funny, and then I started laughing with him. He said, "Honey, you and I are so ridiculously anal when it comes to travel and time management. How did neither one of us think to double-check our departure time?"

I didn't really have a good answer for him, but I think it was just one wedding detail that fell through the cracks.

Luckily, the attendant was able to get us on the next flight, coach rather than first class, and we happily took it. Before we left the check-in station, Tim asked if this was going to change anything for our return flight. The attendant assured us that everything would stay the same for our flight home, but Tim wanted to be really sure. He asked her to double-check it in the computer, which she did. She looked up our return flight and said that this change in our departure flight would absolutely not change anything about our return flight. Reassured, Tim and I left to go through security.

The rest of the trip was amazing. We talked about the details of our wedding nonstop, we laughed more than ever before, and we didn't want to do anything but spend time together. I felt like my heart was getting bigger and bigger and bigger, trying its best to contain the sheer joy I was experiencing, and at any moment it might explode. That sounds painful, but it wasn't; it was delightful.

We ate and drank our way through Maui. We also played golf one day, but mainly, we just consumed delicious food every opportunity we had (if you're ever going to Maui, hit me up on Twitter, and I'll plan out your meals for you) and approximately 47,452 Mai Tais. That is obviously an exaggeration—give or take 1,000.

On October 27, 2013, our honeymoon officially came to an end. We said good-bye to our gorgeous resort and made our way to the airport—after we stopped and had pancakes with peanut butter (amazing—stop everything and try it now) and SPAM and eggs. We walked over to the check-in counter, and Tim said sarcastically, "Uh, sorry, Mr. and Mrs. Belusko, but you've missed your flight." I laughed and told him to not even joke like that. I loved being in Maui, but now that we were on our way home, I was *ready* to get home. We handed the attendant our licenses and stood there patiently. And then . . .

ATTENDANT: Excuse me. Did you guys have any issues on your way out here?

ME: Uh, we missed our first flight out here because I screwed up the times, but the attendant at LAX assured us that it wouldn't change anything for our return flight.

ATTENDANT: Oh, I see. Well, I have good news and bad news.

Tim and I looked at each other, panicked. I suddenly felt like those pancakes with peanut butter were about to leave my body in one way or another.

ME: You can still get us on the flight but we'll be flying coach?

ATTENDANT: Oh, no, I was able to get you in first class *and* on your original flight. The seats just aren't together right now, but that won't be a big deal to change at the gate.

Was he *kidding* me? *Good* news? That was supercalifragilis-ticexpialidocious-ly amazing news! We were on our way home as happy husband and wife, a slightly fatter but no less happy husband and wife, and it was worth every delicious calorie.

CHAPTER 10

THE POOP WHISPERER

Do you follow me on Twitter yet? Well, if you do, (1) *bravo!* and (2) you may have figured out by now that I am obsessed with dogs. I absolutely love my dogs, other people's dogs, rescue dogs, hot dogs, it doesn't matter.

My family got our first dog when I was eight years old. My mom had fallen in love with an adorable long-haired Chihuahua in a local pet store, and immediately my brother and I were hooked. Soon after, we started "Operation: Get Dad On Board" and began begging him to let this furry friend join our family. My dad wasn't opposed to us getting a dog. He just, like a lot of men, wanted a bigger one. You know, the kind of dog he could play fetch with and go for runs with versus the kind that are frequently mistaken for large rats.

Luckily for us, he agreed that we could take this tiny golden one-and-a-half-pound furball home with us, and we were ecstatic. My dad's only caveat was that *he* would get to name our new pooch. I thought our puppy looked like a Justin, or a Bruce, or a Nintendo (as in the kid I had a crush on in third grade, Springsteen, and the best video-game console ever, all of which happened to be favorites of mine in 1989), but my dad didn't agree.

He named our adorable little fluff-muffin, Tyson. As in Evander-Holyfield-ear-biting Mike Tyson. Now, Mr. Tyson hadn't eaten anyone's ear off yet in 1989. He was a relatively new but clearly dominating figure in the world of professional boxing. I guess my dad figured if he couldn't have a manly dog, he could at least have a manly named long-haired Chihuahua.

When I moved out of my parents' house at eighteen, I felt rather lonely. I had a fantastic roommate, but she traveled a lot, and I was home alone more than I ever had been before. Even though I was busy working on the seventh season of *Boy Meets World*, I decided I wanted to have a dog of my own. And that's when I met Anna.

I bought Anna at a pet store before I knew that most pet-store dogs come from puppy mills and that rescuing an animal was a much better alternative. I went into a back room with five little dogs: two Yorkshire terriers, two Maltese terrier pups, and one Chihuahua. Four of the dogs didn't seem to care that I was there. The Yorkies wouldn't give me the time of day, because barking at people who were walking by was apparently more fun—and actually, if you try barking at people, it is pretty enjoy-

My beautiful Anna basking in the sun.

able. The Chihuahua did circles while trying to chase its tail, and one of the Maltese dogs took a quick pee-pee in the corner. Delightful.

You can understand why I wasn't convinced that they were the pooches for me. But Maltese number two, who looked like a fluff of cotton, walked her tiny one-pound body over to my lap. I put my hand under her butt, and she walked up my chest and over to my neck. She curled into a little ball and fell asleep with my hand under her body. She chose me, and I promised to give her a life filled with cuddles, toys, good food, and a warm bed.

I also gave her a name that was fit for a princess: Annastacia Blanca Fishel. Although that was her official name, I only ever called her Anna, or one of the many nicknames she acquired over the years. (Like Mashoogana, Stinks, Nana Banana, and Poop Skittle. Don't ask me about that last one. I have no idea.) My mom eventually added Browna to Anna's official middle name, because she had typical Maltese tear stains that streaked down her face. Annastacia Blanca Browna Fishel: the tiniest dog with the longest name.

I took Anna home with me and fairly quickly discovered many things about her. She loved to lie on my legs, on her back, and have her belly scratched. When I would stop scratching, she would put her two front paws together and wave them up and down, begging for more. She was incessant, and God forbid I needed to change the channel on the television and had to stop for one second. And Anna loved people, especially strangers. If she had never met you before, she wanted to get to know you *really* well. She did this by trying to shove her tongue all the way up your nose. Like a Roto-Rooter drain-cleaning service, she would help clean you out, whether you wanted it or not. She also peed when she got excited. I'd come home from the grocery store, and the minute she saw me, she'd start doing spins and peeing at the same time. Did I mention I had white carpet at the time? My carpet had spiral stains all over it by the time I moved out. Sorry, landlord!

Anna became my little partner in crime. She came to the *Boy Meets World* set with me even though pets weren't allowed on the lot. Kindly, most security guards turned a blind eye to us. Ridiculously, she went to movie premieres with me, where she'd go potty on a pee pad I brought for her. She was a natural model. She loved to have her picture taken, and we did several photo shoots together. When she was full-grown, she weighed eight pounds, but when Anna looked into the mirror, she saw a lioness. She was tough, resilient, always energetic, and not supergirly. She didn't like it when I put bows in her hair, so I didn't do it. She refused to stay clean after a bath and opted to roll in dirty grass almost immediately. Begrudgingly, I always let her. She heard all of my deepest secrets and saw all of my mistakes and never hesitated to love me anyway. She had horrible breath despite getting her teeth cleaned twice a year. I called her my fur baby, and my mom called her "granddogger."

When she was eleven, I did a charity event called Race for the Rescues. The event was at a huge park, and Anna and Tim came with me. It was a 5K and 10K race that raised money for an organization that brought rescued animals into a no-kill shelter until they found loving homes. Another purpose of the event was to adopt out as many animals to new families as possible. There were dogs everywhere, and they all needed homes.

I had absolutely zero intention of adopting another dog. Anna had been sick with kidney disease for a few years and required a lot of medical attention. Plus, she had been an only fur baby for so long I didn't know how she'd react to another fur baby joining our family.

But then I saw this ridiculously small dog. I'm a total sucker for anything small. His two front paws were shaved, and his tongue was hanging out of his miniature mouth. Adorably, he was wearing a bright orange handkerchief that said "Adopt Me!" He was simply too precious for words, and without thinking, I ran over to him and picked him up. There was a woman holding his leash, and I discovered her name was Claudia and that she was his foster mommy.

This little dude's name was Spike, he was around eleven years old, and he had just had surgery to remove all of his teeth. When he was rescued from the pound, his teeth and mouth were horribly infected. He also wasn't neutered, so they had done that surgery at the same time. Basically, Spike had been through a lot recently.

Without even thinking to ask if he was nice, I kissed the side of his face. Claudia's eyes got big, and she said, "Oh. I'm really surprised he let you do that. Let's just say he has a quirky personality." I was instantly hooked. He was just like me: miniature, quirky, and old. I wanted him. I just needed to get Tim and Anna to feel the same way.

Clearly, I would never have adopted a dog that didn't get along with Anna. She was sick, and she needed to be my priority. Tim was running in the race, so I introduced Anna to Spike while I waited for him. I would love to say that it was love at first sight between them, but truthfully, they were totally uninterested in each other. No fighting, no playing, no nothing. They barely even acknowledged each other's presence. That was good enough for me!

When Tim got back from the race, I introduced him to Spike. I would also love to say that it was love at first sight between *them*, but it was actually the opposite. Where Spike was completely apathetic about Anna, he was very passionate about his distaste for Tim. Spike started growling at him, and he wasn't exactly warm and cuddly. Not a good first impression. Tim couldn't possibly fathom what it was I found so endearing

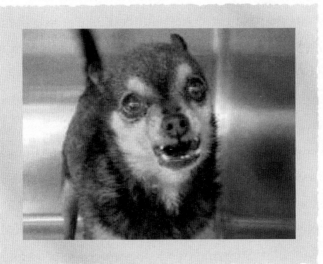

The only photo I own of Spike with teeth. He was at the pound about to be put down when this photo was taken.

about this grumpy old jerk. But it was too late. I was in love. And I wasn't going to rest until he was *my* grumpy old jerk.

We took Spike into our home for a "two-week practice trial." Claudia, his previous foster mommy, gave us a run-down on Spike's habits and quirks. "He's totally healthy, especially for an eleven-year-old," she said as she gave us copies of his most recent veterinary checkup. Indeed, he was healthy. "He isn't super-fond of men, and we think he may have been abused. Just go slow with him." She concluded, "You have two weeks to decide if he is a good fit for your family."

On the first night, Spike wouldn't let us come anywhere near him. He bit us with his toothless gums, which was still surprisingly painful, and it's impossible to not recoil from an angry dog that wants to taste your flesh. He growled at us and refused to eat. He literally wanted nothing to do with us and looked for Claudia for hours after she left. I cried all night. "What have I done?" I said out loud to no one in particular at least five times.

Anna was the only one Spike could bear. He seemed very comfortable with her, and she never elicited a growl or a bark from him. She was very slow around him, though. Anna was a very hyper dog, but for some reason, she knew she had to be calm with him. She would do a doggie version of a tiptoe over to Spike's face and lean in to smell him. Anna really liked the way Spike's ears smelled, and Spike actually let her smell them without putting up a fight.

When it was time to go to sleep, I put the brand-new dog bed I had purchased for Spike earlier in the day on the leather recliner I have in my bedroom. I gingerly picked up Spike and placed him in the bed. He seemed happy there. From his bed, he could see us in our bed, but he was relaxed knowing we weren't going to try to touch him or play with him for a while. Tim and I discussed the events of the evening through my tears. He consoled me with the fact that this *was* Spike's first night in a new place with new people. He was probably just scared, and he would warm up to us over the next few days.

Tim was wrong. For three straight days, Spike made it abundantly clear that he didn't really like us. Actually, I was yet to see anyone he did like. Spike wasn't exactly warm and fuzzy with Claudia, either, and she had been living with him for a few months.

Spike was so darn irresistible! Why didn't he want me to love him and hug him and cuddle him to death? I'm really not a big crier, but I continued to cry for days. What was I going to do if he never warmed up to me? I kept reminding Tim that we had a two-week trial period, so if things didn't get better, we could always give him back to Claudia. The only problem was that this was a total lie. I was never going to give this little man back. I knew the minute he walked into my home that he was never leaving. I didn't care if he bit me a thousand times a day; he was stuck with me for however long he lived.

I knew that I was Spike's last chance for a happy home. He was mean and old and couldn't be trusted around children.

Unfortunately, he was pretty unadoptable to anyone with common sense. Luckily for him, I had none.

Over the next few weeks, Spike and Anna became best friends. They cuddled on the couch together, they took walks side-by-side, and they shared toys. In the next few months, Spike warmed up to me, too. He let me pick him up and scratch his chest. He even started whining in the middle of the night until I picked him up out of his bed and put him in bed with Anna, Tim, and me. He'd cuddle up right next to my side and sleep soundly all night. But with Tim? Let's just say Spike and Tim were in a permanent duel. Spike was the one who took off his white glove and slapped Tim across the face. Side note: How cute would a dog in little white gloves be? I would never do it to my own dogs, but I may have to Google that image.

This is what came up. Not what I was looking for but . . . are you kidding me with this cuteness?

After six months of having Spike, he got sick. He was screaming in pain and wouldn't eat his food. He also couldn't go "number two." I felt terrible for him. Poor little guy was hunched over with terrible stomach spasms. He was also very itchy, and when I scratched certain parts of his back, he winced. I immediately took him to our veterinarian, Dr. Jang, who said he needed to do an ultrasound to find out what was wrong with Spike's stomach cramps. They shaved his little belly and ran a bunch of tests. It turned out that Spike had irritable bowel syndrome (IBS), which causes immense stomach cramping, constipation, and possibly diarrhea. He also had chronic pancreatitis, and it was allergies that were making him itchy. We had to put Spike on several medications for the stomach cramping, one of which was a steroid, and an antihistamine and enzymes for the allergies. Eventually, he got better . . . for a short time.

Within a few months, Spike started drinking a ton of water and needing to pee constantly. I worried that he had kidney disease, because incessant drinking and peeing were the warning signs I had when Anna got sick. Once again, we made our way into the vet's office. Dr. Jang ran some blood tests, and we discovered that Spike had diabetes on top of his IBS, chronic pancreatitis, and allergies. The worst part is that the steroid that helped to control his pancreatitis and IBS wasn't compatible with insulin. Unfortunately, the steroid was the most effective medicine to help regulate his bowels and stop the cramping. We chose to try out a safer but less effective medication and see how he did.

Now I had one dog with kidney disease that required sub-cutaneous fluids twice a week and five medications a day and a second dog with a laundry list of other health issues. On top of being enrolled in college full-time and working thirty-five hours a week hosting a show at night, I was owner, president, and CEO of Fishel Doggie Elder Care.

I had no social life. I planned my school schedule around being able to take care of my dogs and work. I had to learn how to give Grumpy McGrumperson (one of Spike's many nicknames) his insulin shots twice a day. This will totally surprise you (no, it won't), but he didn't like that very much. The first few days were torturous for both of us, because he tried to bite my hand off every morning, and I usually barely got any insulin under his skin.

One particularly exhausting morning started after getting very little sleep the night before. I had an eight o'clock class and had been up since six. I tried to bribe Spike with a piece of cheese so I could sneak-attack him with the insulin injection. I failed miserably. He spun around and snapped at me with his toothless gums, and I panicked. I ripped my right hand, the one holding the needle that injects the insulin, away from his back and out of harm's way very quickly.

I was like a ninja—a stupid ninja who proceeded to stab her-self in the left hand with a super-sharp needle full of insulin. It hurt, I was bleeding, but there was no time to think about that. I was running late for school, and Spike didn't get *his* dose of insulin because I had just inadvertently given it to myself.

As much as I hated to do it, I put Spike in a muzzle and gave him his shot. Right before I ran out the door, I decided I should look up what the consequences were when a nondiabetic person took insulin. It probably wasn't anything too serious, but it couldn't hurt to check, right?

This was the first thing that came up in my Google search: "CAUTION, CAUTION. Insulin taken by a nondiabetic will reduce the person's blood glucose to very low. Unneeded insulin shots will lower blood sugar to a level that can cause coma or death."

Well, that wasn't comforting. I drove to school and walked into class. The second my professor arrived, I walked up to him and said, "Hi. I accidentally gave myself a dose of insulin this morning, and I am not diabetic. Please watch out for any warning signs of me lapsing into a coma or dying. It wasn't too much insulin, by the way. Just enough for a four-pound dog. I'm sure I'll be fine. Thanks for looking out for me."

As you can see, I did indeed live. I hope you weren't too scared while reading that. I can't imagine a world without me, or this book, either. Anyway, Spike eventually learned to take his insulin injection like a champ, no muzzling required. He still needed a cheese bribe, but who would be stupid enough to pass up cheese, like, ever?

One morning, after waking up and going to the bathroom, I came back to the side of the bed to take Spike downstairs and noticed something on our white sheets that wasn't there the night before. There were brown spots. And streaks. Instantly, I checked Spike's butt. A hot, juicy strand of poop was dangling out of his rear end. He was inches away from my pillow and couldn't have been more asleep. I'm obviously not a dog, but I gotta tell ya, if that were me, I would *not* be sleeping soundly. Spike? He was snug as a bug in a rug.

I walked over to Tim's side of the bed. "Babe," I said in a hushed tone. "Look at that," and I pointed to the stains on the bed.

He woke up and rubbed his eyes. He looked at the stains. He looked at them closer. "Oh, my God! Danielle, I didn't do that! Those aren't from me," he said in a complete panic.

"Ugh, *of course* they're not from you," I said.

Before I could tell him what was going on with Spike, he interrupted me. "Did you do that?"

My mouth dropped open. Then I replied, "Did I poop the bed and then wake you up to show you the stains? Is that really what you're asking me right now? We sleep with two dogs in our bed, and your first thought when you see poop stains on the sheets is that they must be from *one of us*?"

Another vet visit and five hundred dollars later, we found out that Spike's IBS and pancreatitis were flaring up and his intestines weren't cooperating. He had also lost control of his anal sphincter. You read that right. His anal sphincter wasn't contracting. Lovely!

Dr. Jang told us that he was going to send Spike home with a few more medications that might help with his poopy-butt problem. In the meantime, since Spike didn't have any control over his butthole, Dr. Jang recommended that we get him some doggie diapers. Since Spike was always such a ~~jerk~~ delight and ~~impossible to please~~ easy to deal with, this was going to ~~suck big time~~ be so adorable!

Miniature dog diapers are actually quite cute. They have a hole cut out in the back for a dog tail and in every other way look like a newborn baby's diaper. Trying to put one on Spike— *not cute.* I'd try to put it on him, and he'd slam his butt to the ground and try to bite me. But what were my options? Live with a dog who had a constant stream of runny poo falling out of his leaky sphincter or make him wear a diaper?

I opted to live with a dog who had a constant stream of runny poo falling out of his leaky sphincter. He refused to wear a diaper, and when I was finally able to get one on him, he wiggled out of it anyway. I decided to cover my couch and my bed with disposable doggie pee pads. I knew I was also going to have to take Spike out for walks a lot more often.

When I'm at home in the morning, I have a routine that I rarely divert from. I wake up, put on a hideous fluffy pink fleece robe, and go downstairs. I take the dogs out for a walk—in my robe. I have no shame. Am I supposed to wake up and immediately get dressed for the day just to walk my dogs? I don't think so. My neighbors have seen me in my robe more often than they've ever seen me put together, and they probably think I am a giant slob, even though the truth is that I actually am a giant slob.

About three days into Spike's sphincter problem, he started to get better. His poops had started to solidify again, but now he seemed to be struggling with minor constipation. I walked him around the block, and we ended up in front of my neighbor's house. Spike got into poop position and started pushing. Something was trying to come out, but it was stuck to his butt. I got a little closer to inspect the problem (did I tell you how much I love dogs yet?).

He had a piece of my hair mixed in with his doo-doo, and he couldn't push it out. I covered my hand with my biodegradable dog-poop bag and squatted to the ground in my pink robe. I reached for Spike's butt, and he growled at me. I grabbed the poop mixed with my hair and pulled the long, stringy, smelly mess out while Spike kept turning around trying to bite me . . . at exactly the same moment that my neighbor, the one whose lawn we were occupying, walked out of his house.

"Hiiiieeee," I said. "Really sorry about this, but Spike here is having some pooping issues. That's probably too much information, right?" I laughed.

He didn't say anything. He just stood there.

"OK, well, we're gonna head back across the street now. Promise I picked everything up . . . not much is coming out of him these days anyway. Sorry, I don't know why I can't stop talking. 'Bye."

I've seen that neighbor multiple times since then. He's always been very nice, and we've never discussed that day when he innocently walked out of his home to find a neighbor in a huge pink robe, crouched on his lawn, pulling dog poop out of her dog's butt. That's probably for the best.

And with that, I leave you with another by-product of Spike's poopy bottom. Sneak attacks when you aren't looking.

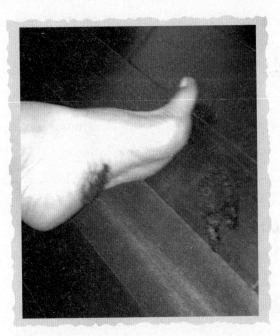

I can't believe I waited to wash my foot so I could take a picture of this. But how do you not share this with people?

CHAPTER 11

I WANT TO BE A RAPPER

Like all young, white, upper-middle-class girls, I grew up wanting to be one of two things: a waitress or a rapper. I'm pretty sure all little girls grow up with that same dream. No? Just me? Whatever.

Looking back, I realize that these goals were a little misguided. For one, I was probably the world's first actress who wanted to be a waitress and not the other way around. And sadly, I was not blessed with the ability to write rhymes. (Even if I were, I'm pretty sure no one would have cared to hear the trials and tribulations of growing up in a well-adjusted family who lived in Orange County during the '80s.) But that didn't stop me from trying—in my own way.

I became obsessed with rap music at a very young age. While most of my friends were into rock and pop music, I was fanatical about Tupac, Notorious B.I.G., Snoop Doggy Dog (that was my favorite of his names), and Eminem. I would anxiously anticipate their album release dates, buy them on the first day, and then immediately memorize all of the lyrics. Truthfully, not much has changed, because I still do that to this day, even though '90s rap will forever be my favorite.

In the late '90s (it may have been 2000—I don't remember dates very well), I was asked to be a celebrity contestant on MTV's *Say What Karaoke*. For those of you who don't remember, *Say What Karaoke* was a show where contestants would sing along to songs for a panel of celebrity judges. Sometimes the contestants were decent, and sometimes they were dreadful, which made it fun to watch. My first instinct was to scream "No!" and run for the hills, because I am not a terrific singer and, therefore, only sing in the car with my music turned up so loudly *I* can't even hear me. But before I turned MTV down, I asked to see the catalog of songs they would allow the contestants to perform and I saw that Busta Rhymes's new song "Gimme Some More" was on the list. I was sold.

I immediately started memorizing the lyrics and practicing Busta Rhymes's super-fast speed. After a couple of days of studying, I felt totally comfortable with my progress, and I couldn't wait for my opportunity to feel like a rapper onstage.

A few weeks later, it was time to tape the segment. The night before I was set to perform, the producers sent me a package. Inside was the schedule for the following day and the clean "Gimme Some More" lyrics. Because I am a total moron, I hadn't thought about the fact that there were words in that song that I obviously wouldn't be allowed to say on national television. Looking at the clean version, I barely even recognized the song. I was going to have to spend all night rememorizing lyrics to a song that didn't give you any wiggle room for mistakes. I was a nervous wreck.

The next day was a blur. I don't remember the whole process, because it all happened so fast, but I do know that I made it to the final round with Ahmet Zappa and Sarah Hagen, Samm Levine, and John Daley from *Freaks and Geeks*. If my memory serves correctly, Ahmet was performing a Britney Spears song, and the *Freaks and Geeks* kids did Smashmouth's "Allstar."

When it was my turn to perform, I put my earpiece in, and the music started. The audience began screaming so loudly that I couldn't hear anything in my headset, and it was of no help to me. I knew I was going to have to rap based strictly on what I had memorized and rehearsed. I wanted to do a great job and come out victorious, but I felt like I might throw up instead.

Fortunately, I managed to keep my lunch down, but I didn't get off to a great start. I started rapping the opening lyrics one second too early, which meant I rapped *faster* than Busta Rhymes through the entire song. Certainly not an easy feat, but it also didn't win me any points. Ahmet Zappa claimed the victory and the prize, which was a snowboard. Backstage, everyone was very kind to me and told me what an amazing job I had done. All I knew was that I had failed myself and that I needed to put my dreams of rap stardom behind me.

For the rest of the weekend, everywhere I went, people would ask me about my performance and tell me how much they enjoyed it. It felt awesome, and I started to think that maybe I hadn't been such a failure after all. On my last day at the hotel, I was walking toward the elevator, when a stranger yelled "Gimme Some More!" in my direction. Happy that someone had clearly appreciated my rap skills, I smiled and yelled "Gimme Some More!" right back— but someone else said it at the same time. I turned around to see who was trying to steal my spotlight and saw Busta Rhymes standing in the elevator holding the door for me. He was there to be a part of MTV's "Spring Break," and it was in that moment that I realized that the stranger was not yelling "Gimme Some More!" at me but at the far superior Busta. I bowed my head in embarrassment and stepped onto the elevator.

"Hey, I saw your performance yesterday. Pretty tight," said the only man who was also on the elevator with Busta and me. "I'm Spliff."

I immediately knew that Spliff was Spliff Star, because Busta mentioned him in "Gimme Some More," and being a giant fan, I had looked him up. Apparently, he didn't think I would believe him, even though Busta was in the elevator with us, because in order to prove he wasn't lying, he lifted his shirt over his head to show me his huge tattoo that spelled "Spliff" across the top of his back.

"Oh, great. I'm a big fan, so I'm really embarrassed that I rapped it too fast," I said.

Busta started laughing. "I didn't get to see it, but any little girl who can rap faster than me is all right."

I smiled as he and Spliff got off the elevator.

It's been nearly fifteen years since that performance, and I have never watched it. I was too embarrassed at the time it aired to try to catch a rerun of the episode. For some reason, there isn't a video of it anywhere online, but I would love to watch it now.

I knew that (brief) moment of (partial) glory on MTV was as close as I would ever come to being a professional rapper and decided it was time to hang that dream up for good. But I had no way of knowing that just a few years later, I would become a "wrapper."

In October 2006, I got an invitation to the wedding of my former *Boy Meets World* costar, Maitland Ward. I went to Bloomingdale's at eight o'clock the night before the wedding to get a gift, because, like an idiot, I had waited until the last minute. I picked out some gorgeous wineglasses from the couple's registry and asked to have them gift-wrapped. When I went to the customer service department, where they did the wrapping, there was one girl working behind the counter and no one in line. *Perfect*, I thought. I knew Bloomingdale's closed at nine, but wrapping one present shouldn't take too much time.

"Hi. Can I please have this gift-wrapped?" I said to the sweet-looking girl behind the counter. "Sure. What time do you want to pick it up tomorrow?" she asked.

ME: I'm sorry. I can't pick it up tomorrow, because this is a wedding present, and the wedding is tomorrow.

HER: Oh. Um, well, I can't do it right now.

ME: Why? Are you wrapping other presents?

HER: No. But I just closed the registers.

ME: I thought you closed at nine?

HER: We do. But we're really slow, and I didn't think anyone else would be coming in, so I just decided to count my registers early so I can leave right at nine.

ME: Hmm. OK. Any chance you can just rip off some paper and hand me your scissors and some tape and I'll wrap it myself?

HER: Sure.

She ripped off a big piece of wedding wrapping paper and handed it to me. I sat down on the floor and got to work. A few minutes later, a store manager walked by, saw me on the floor, and gasped. "What are you *doing*?" I didn't want to get the girl in trouble, so I explained that I really liked to wrap presents and wanted to do it myself. He told me that they had a very strict policy not to let customers wrap their own gifts, and at that point, the girl behind the counter chimed in with some attitude directed toward me.

HER: Actually, I told her she could come back *tomorrow* to pick up her gift, but she said she needed it wrapped *tonight*.

MANAGER: So why didn't you wrap it tonight?

HER: Uhh . . . because I already closed the registers.

MANAGER: You closed the registers? But it's only eight thirty.

At this point, things were starting to get awkward, and I had finished wrapping my present. I stood up and said, "Thank you guys for your help. Sorry I was a bit of a pest."

The manager apologized profusely for his employee and handed me a box of complimentary chocolates for my trouble. He looked down and noticed my wrapped gift and said, "Wow. You did that very well. You know, if you want a job, we hire people around Christmas strictly to wrap presents!"

I told him that actually sounded like fun and I might take him up on it. He handed me his business card, and I left.

For the next few days, I contemplated the idea of wrapping presents at Bloomingdale's. I wasn't working at the time, so it wasn't like I wouldn't be able to find the time in my schedule, and I *did* enjoy wrapping presents. After mulling it over for a couple of weeks, I couldn't think of a downside, so I called the number on the manager's card, and he connected me to the human resources department. I made an appointment to go talk with them and find out more details.

A few days later, I was sitting in my first-ever interview for a nonacting job, or what I call a real job. The human resources manager told me that contrary to what I had been previously told, I could not work for Bloomingdale's strictly as a gift wrapper. I was going to have to learn all about customer service and be trained. Even though that sounded like a downside, I agreed to work there part-time for two months and see how it went.

After a few days of horribly boring computer training, I was ready to start my first day. I was told that we had to wear all black, so I put on my favorite black pencil skirt and a black silk blouse, but I thought my outfit needed a splash of color, so I wore my favorite pair of bright red heels.

I got to work, clocked in, and said hello to the people I would be working with. The first person I met was the girl who had given me the opportunity for this job by closing her registers early a few weeks before. She was very nice, but there was a little awkwardness between us, because (I assumed) she recognized me as the girl who got her in trouble with her manager. I never did tell anyone about how I got the idea to start working there, because I'm not a gossip, but I did keep my eye on her. I obviously had a fairly good reason to be skeptical about her work ethic.

When it was time for lunch, I went to the break room to heat up the soup I had brought with me from home. I saw a woman eyeing my shoes and thought, *Good choice, Danielle.* She walked over to me, introduced herself as the general manager, and asked which department I worked in. I told her that today was my first day in customer service, and she said, "Well, I guess that explains it. Our all-black dress code means just that—all black. No red shoes tomorrow, please." Do I know how to impress the bosses or what?

I have a lot of great memories from my time at Bloomingdale's, but my favorite stories are about how rude people can be. Like the guy who walked to my counter in a rage because he said he paid his Bloomingdale's card off every month so he didn't understand why his bill said "Available credit: $5,000." I explained to him that that meant he had *$5,000 worth of credit* and he could spend up to $5,000 before he hit his spending limit. I also showed him where his balance due said $0.00. This didn't make any sense to him, and he screamed at me that I was "an effing degenerate who didn't know how to read." I'm sure it goes without saying that he did *not* use the word *effing*—he used the real word. It was the first time a stranger had ever screamed an obscenity at me, and despite my shock, I couldn't help but be kind of excited to have a great "working in retail" story!

The idiot, I mean, man, asked to speak with my manager, so I went into the back room to get her. She calmly walked over to him and explained his bill to him the same way I had. He still didn't quite understand what she was saying, but he eventually walked away. I stood there with the biggest smile on my face, just to tick him off.

There was also the time a woman jumped across the counter, grabbed me by my jacket lapels, and started shaking me. A couple of times a year, Bloomingdale's offers $25 coupons for every $100 you spend, not including tax. It's a great deal, and a lot of people spend thousands of dollars to take advantage of the discount. Unfortunately, these sales make life miserable for everyone who works in the store. In order to get the coupons, Bloomingdale's employees have to check every receipt for every customer from every department and calculate their total minus tax.

One night, when the store was jam-packed with people who had a lust for $25 coupons, a woman named Michelle approached my counter, and I could tell she was furious. She told me that the previous evening, "a stupid little girl downstairs" had added up her receipts incorrectly and shortchanged her several coupons. I told her that I was terribly sorry for her inconvenience and I would recalculate her total and fix the problem. Michelle handed me her receipts and all of the $25 coupons she had been given the night before.

I pulled out my calculator and started adding up the totals of her receipts, remembering to subtract the sales tax. When I was done, I counted the number of cards she had been given and discovered that despite what Michelle claimed, she had actually been given one card too many.

I put Michelle's coupons on the counter and showed her my calculator, which displayed her total spent, minus sales tax. Michelle demanded to know where it was stated that sales tax didn't count toward her total, so I showed her.

> ME: Michelle, I'm very sorry you weren't aware that sales tax wasn't included, but if it makes you feel any better, you weren't shortchanged any coupons—you actually got one more than you should have!

I had absolutely *no* intention of taking away Michelle's extra coupon. I wasn't the employee who had made the mistake, and if Michelle hadn't come into our store to complain, we never would have known she had been given too many. But apparently, Michelle didn't pick up on that. Wild-eyed, she looked at her coupons, still in my hand, and leaped into the air, flat on her stomach onto the top of my counter. She grabbed me by the lapels of my jacket and shook me violently while screaming, "Give me my coupons!" Terrified, I threw her coupons into the air, and she scooped them up off the ground the way a rabid dog that hadn't seen a meal in weeks would attack a ribeye.

To this day, I'm afraid of coupons.

I enjoyed my time at Bloomingdale's so much I even went back to do it again the following year. They had great sales, and the employee discount was fantastic, so I may or may not have lost money while working for them (whoops). But I met some wonderful people, and it was fun to wrap beautiful gifts that our customers had lovingly bought for their friends and family.

Please, do me a favor, and always be polite to the dear souls who work in the service industry. They work long, thankless hours, usually on their feet, and sometimes they're even forced to wear all black—no pops of color allowed, even if that pop of color is a gorgeous pair of red heels! So don't be a jerk. It's really gross and disgusting. Plus, you never know when a famous wrapper will call you out in her book.

ACKNOWLEDGMENTS

Although I wrote this book alone, it would not have been possible without the love and support of countless people. Thank you to "Mr. Husband," Tim, for his encouragement, dedication, love, and willingness to let me share a part of our lives with the world. To my parents, Jennifer Fishel and Rick Fishel, for teaching me my most treasured qualities: good values, discipline, humor, and compassion. To my brother, Chris, who made sacrifices so that I could do *Boy Meets World* and still loves me despite having been called "Topanga's brother" more than a few times. Thank you to my grandparents, Papa Joey and Amma and Papa Fishel, for their never-ending support and to my friends Jamie, Brandy, and Danielle for continuing to inspire me when I feel overwhelmed. Thank you to everyone who provided me with personal pictures, including Tim Hart, Claudia Perrone, Sarah Uphoff, and Ashley Concolino.

The Beluskos, Mike, Lisa, Lauren, Grandma and Grandpa, and Nanny, thank you for welcoming me into your family and for loving me, "warts and all." To Rider Strong, Will Friedle, and the rest of my *Boy Meets World* family, you helped shape the most influential years of my life and I am a better person because of it. To my *Girl Meets World* family, I am so proud of every one of you and am thankful to have you in my life. Finally, my deepest gratitude to Michael Jacobs and Ben Savage for giving me the opportunity of a lifetime and for your treasured friendship and guidance.

Thank you to Gallery Books for believing in me and for easily being the most fun people to sit with in a meeting. To my editor Emilia Pisani, thank you for your excellent advice and expeditious turnaround time. You know I like people who are good with time management! To my second and equally wonderful editor, Kate Dresser, thank you for your patience and understanding when I made approximately 1000 changes at the last minute. To the most spectacular managers in the universe, Ray Moheet and Reg Tigerman, thank you for your tireless dedication and for never being mad at me when I tell you to pass on nearly everything that comes my way. No one has ever worked harder for me than you and I am eternally grateful. Thank you to Paul Mobley for shooting the cover and being so fun to work with. Thank you to Julie Cuomo for being a genius with makeup, Laurie Heaps for your mastery with a curling iron, and

Nicole Gorsuch for hoarding such beautiful vintage dresses for me to wear.

Last but not least, a sincere thank you to all of you who have supported my career over the years. Without you, I wouldn't be able to do what I love, and therefore, you have given me a priceless gift.